Copy Editor & Interior Design: Constance Santego
Book Layout: ©2017 BookDesignTemplates.com

Ordering Information:
Quantity sales. Special discounts are available on quantity purchases by corporations, associations, and others. For details, contact the "Special Sales Department" at the address above.

Trade Paperback ISBN: 978-1-997907-06-0
Ebook ISBN 978-1-997907-07-7
Created and published In Canada. Printed and bound in the United States of America

First Edition
Published by Maximillian Enterprises
Kelowna, BC Canada
www.constancesantego.ca

Crown Chakra 101: Spiritual Connection, Transcendence.

"Beyond thought, beyond form — into pure being."

(Vol VII)

Dr. Constance Santego

Maximillian Enterprises
Kelowna, BC

Dedication

To those who began at the Heart and ascended through every color of the soul.
May this final light remind you:
you were never separate — you were the divine all along.
— Dr. Constance Santego

ALSO BY DR. CONSTANCE SANTEGO

NOVELS
Illegitimate Grace
Ashcroft Hollow

Okanagan Trilogy:
Beneath the Vineyards
Under the Okanagan Sun
Guardian of the Lake

The Nine Spiritual Gifts Series:
Journey of a Soul – (Vol 1 Michael)
Language of a Soul – (Vol 2 Gabriel)
Prophecy of a Soul – (Vol 3 Bath Kol)
Healing of a Soul – (Vol 4 Raphael)
Miracles of a Soul – (Vol 5 Hamied)
Knowledge of a Soul – (Vol 6 Raziel)
Wisdom of a Soul – (Vol 7 Uriel)
Faith of a Soul – (Vol 8 Pistis Sophia)

NONFICTION
The Intuitive Life, The Gift Of Prophecy, Third Edition
Fairy Tales, Dreams And Reality… Where Are You On Your Path? Second
Edition
Your Persona… The Mask You Wear
Archangel Michael's Soul Retrieval Guide
Tesla And The Future Of Energy Medicine
Beyond Tesla: Advancing The Science Of Energy Healing
Tesla's Code: Mastering Energy, Frequency, And Creative Power
Beyond The Mind: Harnessing The Power Of Astral Projection For Creative
Awakening
Bend, Don't Break: Finding Your Way Back To Abundance
Ring Therapy: A Guide To Healing And Balance
Ring Therapy Pocket Guide
Floraopathy™: The Art And Science Of Vibrational Healing With Essential
Oils
Dear Older Me: A Memoir… Of Sorts
It's Just Like Poker: A Spiritual Guide To Playing The
Cards Life Deals You
Signs And Meanings: What The Feet Reveal About Health, Stress, And The
Body's Story
Auricions: Unlocking Subconscious Healing Through Quantum Medicine
Quick Fix Acupressure Method

Manifestation – The DREAM Method in 5 Steps
Confidence- Mastering the Dream Method

The New Paradigm: Conscious Healing In The Age Of Ai

REIKI WISDOM, SERIES:
Angelic Lifestyle, a Vibrant Lifestyle
Angelic Lifestyle 42-Day Energy Cleanse
Reiki and the Power of The Joint Points: Unlocking Energy Pathways for
Healing (Vol I)
Reiki and Karmic Healing: Releasing Patterns From Past Lives (Vol II)
Reiki and the Five Elements (Vol III)
Secrets of a Healer, Magic Of Reiki
The Reiki Master's Manual

CHAKRA SERIES:
Heart Chakra 101: The Bridge
Root Chakra 101: Building Safety, Survival, Foundation
Sacral Chakra 101: Creativity, Pleasure, Emotions
Solar Plexus Chakra 101: Power, Confidence, Will
Throat Chakra 101: Truth, Voice, Self-Expression
Third Eye Chakra 101: Intuition, Vision, Insight
Crown Chakra 101: Spiritual Connection, Transcendence.

SECRETS OF A HEALER, SERIES:
Magic Of Aromatherapy (Vol I)
Magic Of Reflexology (Vol II)
Magic Of The Gifts (Vol III)
Magic Of Muscle Testing (Vol IV)
Magic Of Iridology (Vol V)
Magic Of Massage (Vol VI)
Magic Of Hypnotherapy (Vol VII)
Magic Of Reiki (Vol VIII)
Magic Of Advanced Aromatherapy (Vol IX)
Magic Of Esthetics (Vol X)
The Reiki Master's Manual (Vol XI)

ADULT COLORING JOURNALS
SERIES-ZEN COLORING:
Quantum Energy and Mindful Living Journal (Vol 1)
Reiki Energy Journal (Vol 2)
Nine Spiritual Gifts Journal (Vol 3)
I Forgive Journal (Vol 4)

FOR CHILDREN
I am Big Tonight. I Don't Need the Light
The Magic Elf Book: 25 Days of Surprises

COOKBOOK
My Favorite Recipes, with a Hint of Giggle

BUISNESS
How To Use ChatGPT For Authors: From Idea To Published Book
Scaling Beyond 6 Figures: Strategies For Health & Wellness Professionals
The Academypreneur's Playbook: Turn Knowledge Into A
Revenue-Generating School

HUMOR/GIFT BOOK
How Do You Like Your Eggs? Crack Into Your Personality, Yolk and All

Contents

Crown Chakra 101: Spiritual Connection, Transcendence.

"Beyond thought, beyond form — into pure being."

(Vol VII)

Dr. Constance Santego

Preface

RETURNING TO THE LIGHT

The journey of awakening comes full circle — ever upward, ever inward — until there is no distinction between ascent and stillness.

From the inner vision of the Third Eye, our awareness now rises beyond perception itself, dissolving into the infinite field of consciousness — the Crown Chakra (Sahasrara), the thousand-petaled lotus of spiritual connection and transcendence.

Here, energy no longer seeks, speaks, or sees. It simply is. The vibration of being replaces the striving of becoming. The individual merges with the infinite, and the light that once illuminated our path now reveals itself as our very essence.

Sahasrara is the culmination of the human and the divine — the meeting point of Heaven and Earth, matter and Spirit, silence and sound. It is not the end of the journey, but the recognition that there never was a journey at all, only the eternal unfolding of consciousness remembering itself.

Its element is beyond elements — neither air nor ether, but pure awareness. Its color is beyond color — white, the merging of all hues, the totality of existence united as one radiant light.

When balanced, the Crown Chakra awakens peace beyond understanding, compassion without condition, and wisdom without words. We live in harmony with the divine order, guided not by thought but by presence. When clouded, we feel separated from Source — adrift in confusion, spiritual doubt, or disconnection from meaning.

Sahasrara is not a destination to reach, but a space to surrender into. It invites us to release every identity, every story, and every boundary that keeps us small. In that surrender, the light of unity dawns — and we awaken not as seekers of the divine, but as expressions of it.

In these pages, we will explore the sacred art of transcendence — how to open to divine consciousness through meditation, Reiki, stillness, and grace. You will learn how the awakening of the Crown completes the circuit of light through all seven chakras, uniting body, mind, and Spirit into wholeness.

As you enter this final realm, remember: enlightenment is not an escape from life but the illumination of it. True transcendence is not leaving the world behind — it is seeing the divine shining through all things.

The Crown Chakra is not above you. It is within you — the light that has been guiding you home all along.

ABOUT THE CHAKRA 101 SERIES

The *Chakra 101 Series* is a journey through the seven primary energy centers of the human body — a path of remembering, where Spirit expresses itself through matter and healing unfolds layer by layer. Each book blends ancient wisdom with modern understanding, bridging spirituality, psychology, and embodied energy practice to guide readers toward balance, awareness, and wholeness.

The journey began with Heart Chakra 101: The Bridge, where love and compassion opened the way for transformation. Root Chakra 101: Building Safety, Survival, Foundation grounded that love into the Earth, teaching trust and belonging.

Sacral Chakra 101: Creativity, Pleasure, Emotions awakened movement, joy, and creation — the rhythm of life flowing through form.
Solar Plexus Chakra 101: Power, Confidence, Will ignited purpose and self-mastery, transforming doubt into radiant action.
Throat Chakra 101: Expression, Authenticity, Truth opened the channel between inner and outer worlds, where vibration became creation.
Third Eye Chakra 101: Intuition, Vision, Insight illuminated the mind with wisdom, guiding us beyond illusion to the clarity of soul.
Now, in Crown Chakra 101: Spiritual Connection, Transcendence, the journey reaches its zenith — where all paths merge into one, and all colors return to light.

Each volume has served as a key, unlocking another facet of consciousness. Together, they form a complete map — a spiral from Earth to sky, from form to formlessness, from self to Source.

This path through the chakras mirrors the sacred rhythm of awakening itself: to love deeply, to ground securely, to create freely, to act with integrity,
to speak with truth,
to see with wisdom,
and finally — to be.

Whether you are a healer, student, or seeker, this final book invites you to rest in the stillness you have been seeking, to dwell in the unity you have always known.

May this be your reminder:
The journey is complete,
the circle unbroken,
the light eternal.

Chapter 1 – The Light of Consciousness

The Role of the Crown Chakra in the Chakra System

Every journey of energy is a movement from Earth to sky, from vibration to silence, from individuality to infinity. After grounding in the Root, flowing through the Sacral, igniting purpose in the Solar Plexus, opening the Heart, expressing truth through the Throat, and awakening vision through the Third Eye — energy now ascends into the Crown Chakra (Sahasrara) — the thousand-petaled lotus of divine connection and transcendence.

Though our series began at the Heart, where love first awakened consciousness, it is here, in the Crown, that consciousness remembers itself as divine. All that we have learned, felt, expressed, and seen culminates in this moment of surrender — the dissolution of form into formlessness, of seeker into Source.

If the Root whispers, *"You are safe,"* the Sacral flows, *"You may feel,"* the Solar Plexus declares, *"You may act,"* the Heart affirms, *"You may love,"* the Throat sings, *"You may speak,"* and the Third Eye reveals, *"You may see,"* then the Crown radiates, *"You are One."*

Sahasrara governs the highest state of awareness — the recognition that the same light animating all creation resides within you. It is not the mind that thinks or the eye that sees, but the pure consciousness behind them both. Here, the self does not seek knowledge; it *is* knowledge — infinite, boundless, eternal.

The Crown's element is beyond all others. It is not Earth, water, fire, air, or even ether — it is pure consciousness itself. Its color is violet fading into white, the merging of all frequencies into one radiant light. Its symbol, the thousand-petaled lotus, represents infinite expansion — the full flowering of spiritual awareness where duality dissolves into unity.

In the chakra system, Sahasrara completes the great spiral of evolution. Without grounding in the Root, awakening here can cause disorientation or detachment. Without the clarity of the Third Eye, spiritual light may scatter into illusion or fanaticism. But when energy flows harmoniously from the Earth to the heavens — through love, truth, and insight — the Crown becomes the radiant halo of illumination, effortlessly linking the individual soul with universal consciousness.

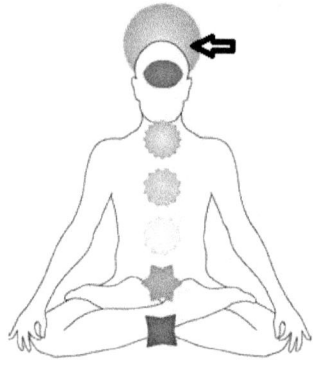

Think of the Crown Chakra as the breath of infinity. The Root anchors life into matter; the Sacral gives it movement; the Solar Plexus gives it will; the Heart fills it with compassion; the Throat gives it sound; the Third Eye gives it vision — and the Crown gives it light. It is the great return — where vibration becomes silence, and silence becomes everything.

When Sahasrara is balanced, you experience clarity, serenity, and profound peace. You no longer seek meaning — you live it. Intuition becomes wisdom, love becomes devotion, and life itself becomes meditation. When blocked, you may feel lost, disconnected from faith or purpose, imprisoned by doubt or mental exhaustion. When overactive, you may drift into escapism or spiritual detachment — seeking the divine while forgetting the human heart that embodies it.

In the great ascent of consciousness, the Crown Chakra represents the will to *surrender.* It is the bridge between the personal and the cosmic — where the drop returns to the ocean, and the ocean recognizes itself in the drop. Sahasrara teaches that enlightenment is not achieved through striving, but revealed through stillness.

Balanced, the Crown Chakra radiates grace, unity, and divine wisdom. Imbalanced, it creates confusion, spiritual emptiness, or isolation. In its highest expression, it becomes the Light of Oneness — the awakened awareness that perceives the sacred in all things.

The Crown invites you to open beyond understanding — to let go of control, to rest in the infinite, to remember that you are not the light's reflection but its source.
For when your consciousness aligns with the divine, thought becomes silence, separation becomes wholeness, and you awaken to the eternal truth:

You are the light — timeless, limitless, and free.

TRADITIONAL SANSKRIT NAMES

Sahasrara (सहस्रार) – The traditional Sanskrit name for the Crown Chakra, meaning *"thousand-petaled."* The term derives from *sahasra*, meaning "a thousand" or "infinite," and *ara*, meaning "spoke" or "petal." Sahasrara symbolizes the infinite expansion of consciousness — the point where individual awareness merges with universal being. It is the lotus of illumination, the crown of spiritual awakening, and the gateway through which divine light flows into the human experience.

In the ancient *Tantric* and *Yogic* texts, Sahasrara is described as a luminous lotus radiating with a thousand white or violet petals — each petal representing a facet of consciousness, a vibration of divine intelligence. This lotus blossoms upward, opening toward the heavens, signifying the soul's return to Source. At its center lies a radiant point of light — the Bindu, or seed of creation — symbolizing the unmanifest reality from which all existence arises and into which all returns.

Sahasrara transcends the physical elements of the lower chakras. While the Root anchors us to Earth and the Third Eye reveals inner vision, the Crown dissolves all form into pure consciousness. It is said to be beyond the five great elements (*Pancha Mahabhutas*) — Earth, water, fire, air, and ether — resting instead in the element of thoughtless awareness, or *mahattattva*, the great principle of universal intelligence.

Associated with the pineal and pituitary glands, Sahasrara regulates the body's endocrine harmony and subtle energy flow, bridging the physical and the spiritual. When awakened, this chakra radiates a serene, blissful light — *Sat-Chit-Ananda* — existence, consciousness, and bliss. It is the moment of realization that the divine one seeks has always been within; that the seeker and the sought are one.

In the *Upanishads*, Sahasrara is revered as the "seat of liberation" (*moksha-sthana*), the supreme state in which the yogi experiences unity with Brahman — the formless Absolute. Here, all boundaries of mind, time, and identity dissolve, leaving only stillness and infinite light. It is not merely awakening but remembrance — the recognition that we have always been what we seek.

Sahasrara purifies through surrender, not striving. It dissolves the ego's attachment to individuality, transforming separation into union and thought into silence. Its activation marks the passage from self-awareness to divine awareness — the realization that consciousness is not something we possess, but what we *are*.

COMMON ENGLISH NAMES

- Crown Chakra – The most recognized English name, referring to its location at the top of the head and its function as the *crown of consciousness.* It symbolizes divine connection, spiritual enlightenment, and the radiant unity of all existence.
- Lotus of a Thousand Petals – Drawn from its Sanskrit meaning, this poetic title expresses the infinite nature of awareness. Each petal represents an aspect of divine wisdom unfolding through the human experience.
- Center of Divine Union – Reflects Sahasrara's role as the meeting point of the human and the eternal. It is where individuality dissolves and the soul merges with the universal field of light.
- Seat of Enlightenment – Emphasizes the Crown's connection to liberation (*moksha*) — the realization of one's true nature as consciousness itself, free from illusion and limitation.
- Bridge to the Infinite – Describes Sahasrara as the final link between the finite and the boundless. It is the bridge that leads beyond birth and death, beyond thought and form.
- Portal of Pure Being – Highlights its transcendental essence — the passage from duality into unity, from doing into being, from self into Source.

Balanced, the Crown Chakra awakens the experience of oneness — a state beyond emotion or thought, where peace is not something attained but simply known. Imbalanced, it manifests as disconnection, doubt, or spiritual emptiness. In its awakened state, Sahasrara becomes the radiant halo of divine consciousness — the eternal light that crowns the soul and illumines all creation.

ETHERIC CHAKRA

Unlike the lower chakras, which correspond to the five great elements — Earth, water, fire, air, and ether — the Crown Chakra (Sahasrara) transcends them all. It is associated not with matter, but with pure consciousness, sometimes called *mahat tattva* — the great principle of universal awareness.
Here, energy no longer moves through form; it becomes the field from which all form arises. It is the realm of the unmanifest — infinite, radiant, and still. The element of the Crown is beyond substance, vibration, or direction. It is the etheric light of being itself, the presence that witnesses all experience without attachment or division.

Within Sahasrara, this transcendental "element" symbolizes unity consciousness — the realization that the light we seek outside is the same light that shines within. It is not illumination as an act, but illumination as existence itself.

CENTER OF DIVINE CONSCIOUSNESS

The Crown Chakra represents *jnana*, or supreme wisdom — knowledge that is not learned but remembered. It is the seat of divine intelligence, where awareness perceives itself as infinite. Just as light reveals all yet remains untouched by what it illuminates, consciousness reveals creation without being altered by it.

Through Sahasrara, we awaken to the truth that perception and reality are one — that what we experience as life is consciousness unfolding itself in infinite forms.

VIOLET–WHITE CHAKRA

Sahasrara is identified by hues of violet, white, and iridescent gold — colors that signify purity, transcendence, and divine radiance. Violet holds the vibration of spiritual awakening and transformation, while white represents the synthesis of all colors — the total spectrum united as one.

These shades are not merely visual but vibrational signatures of enlightenment. Violet bridges Heaven and Earth, inviting the highest frequency of awareness into form. White, the color of cosmic consciousness, embodies the presence that is everything and nothing — the eternal now.

LOTUS OF A THOUSAND PETALS

The sacred symbol of the Crown Chakra is the thousand-petaled lotus, or *Sahasrara Padma*. Each petal represents a vibration, a thought, or a layer of consciousness unfolding from unity into multiplicity. When this lotus is closed, awareness identifies with limitation; when it blooms, the soul returns to its infinite nature.

At the lotus's center rests the Bindu — a radiant point of pure light — symbolizing the divine spark within every being. It is said that through meditation, the thousand petals open one by one, until the self is dissolved into the brilliance of the Absolute. The blooming lotus is not the birth of something new but the revelation of what has always been: the light of the soul in full remembrance of itself.

SEAT OF ENLIGHTENMENT

Sahasrara is often called the *brahmarandhra*, the "opening to Brahman" — the crown of illumination through which divine consciousness enters and exits the body. It is both the summit and the source, the origin and the return.

Here, energy flows both upward and downward — uniting Heaven and Earth, Spirit and matter. The descending current

(*Shakti*) carries grace into the world; the ascending current (*Shiva*) carries awareness back to Source. In balance, they merge into the eternal flow of divine harmony — creation breathing itself.

BRIDGE OF HEAVEN AND EARTH

Serving as the final bridge between the finite and the infinite, Sahasrara connects the embodied self with the universal field. Through this chakra, the individual no longer perceives themselves as separate from life but as life itself — conscious, radiant, divine. When the Crown is open, the mind becomes silent, and the heart becomes the voice of wisdom. Time dissolves into eternity, and the soul remembers its boundless nature. When this connection is weakened, the individual may feel spiritually lost, disconnected from purpose, or adrift in the noise of thought.

Balanced, the Crown Chakra radiates serenity, clarity, and bliss. Awareness expands beyond the boundaries of the personal mind, resting in the vast stillness of being. It teaches that enlightenment is not an attainment but a remembrance — the quiet realization that the light we search for is the essence of who we already are.

The thousand-petaled lotus reminds us:
We are not beneath the divine, but expressions of it — luminous, eternal, and free.

SAHASRARA: THE LOTUS OF LIGHT

The Sanskrit name for the Crown Chakra is Sahasrara (सहस्रार) — a word that means *"thousand-petaled"* or *"infinite expansion."* The term originates from *sahasra*, meaning "a thousand," and *ara*, meaning "spoke" or "petal." Together, these describe not merely a number but a state of boundless consciousness — the radiant unfolding of divine awareness in infinite directions. Sahasrara is the Lotus of Light, the highest seat of consciousness where individuality dissolves into unity and Spirit awakens to its own eternal nature.

If the Third Eye teaches us to perceive, the Crown teaches us to be.
It is the sanctuary of pure awareness — where knowing transcends knowledge, and existence merges with essence. Through Sahasrara, the vibration of OM fades into silence, the soundless source from which all creation arises. It is the still point beyond duality, where every path, every breath, and every thought returns to its origin in divine consciousness.

From the moment self-awareness dawns, the soul begins its pilgrimage home — journeying through matter and mind toward remembrance of its infinite source. The grounding of Muladhara teaches safety, Svadhisthana awakens emotion, Manipura ignites will, Anahata opens love, Vishuddha gives voice to truth, Ajna brings vision — and Sahasrara reveals the light behind them all.
It is not the culmination of awakening, but the realization that awakening never began — that you were always one with the light.

Sahasrara governs the crown of the head, the cerebral cortex, and the subtle connection to the higher self. Energetically, it is the axis of divine intelligence, through which inspiration, grace, and spiritual awareness flow. When this chakra awakens, consciousness expands beyond time and space, perceiving all existence as a single luminous presence.

When Sahasrara is balanced, awareness rests in stillness — not as an absence of thought, but as the presence that witnesses thought. There is peace without reason, love without condition, and clarity without object. The mind no longer seeks to understand the divine; it remembers that it *is* divine.
When imbalanced, we may feel spiritually disconnected,

skeptical, or lost in the noise of intellect. When overactivated, we may drift into escapism or neglect of the body — mistaking transcendence for detachment.

True balance of Sahasrara unites Heaven and Earth within the human heart.

Sahasrara is the sun above suns, the radiant field through which consciousness knows itself as infinite. It draws illumination from the insight of Ajna and distributes that light through every chakra below, creating coherence in the energy body. Without the grounding of the Root and the clarity of the Third Eye, the Crown cannot sustain its brilliance — for divine energy must have a vessel through which to express.

When harmonized, the thousand-petaled lotus blooms effortlessly, and the self dissolves into light.

Sahasrara represents the intelligence of transcendence. It is where the finite meets the infinite — the space in which all separation fades into silence. When this chakra awakens, there is no longer the "seer" and the "seen," only seeing — the pure act of awareness beholding itself.

Just as the sky contains every cloud yet remains untouched by them, Sahasrara encompasses all experience without being defined by it. It is consciousness beyond concept — boundless, luminous, free.

Here, the journey ends not in discovery, but in remembrance. You are not the light's reflection — you are its source. You are not part of the divine — you are its living expression. You are the thousand-petaled lotus, unfolding in every moment of awareness.

It is here, in the violet-white radiance of Sahasrara, that your journey into Spirit, consciousness, and unity begins.

WHAT IS SANSKRIT AND WHY DOES IT MATTER FOR SAHASRARA?

The chakras originate in the sacred language of Sanskrit — a language not merely spoken, but *vibrated.* Sanskrit is often called *Devavāṇī*, "the voice of the gods," because its syllables are living frequencies — energetic codes that awaken consciousness. Each sound is a mantra, a key that opens a specific vibration within the subtle body.

For the Crown Chakra, the Sanskrit name Sahasrara (सहस्रार) embodies the vibration of infinite awareness. The word itself is a mantra of expansion — each syllable invoking the unfolding of consciousness through all layers of being. To speak "Sahasrara" is to invoke remembrance of unity, to awaken the thousand petals of divine light within the crown.

Unlike conventional languages, Sanskrit is a technology of consciousness. Its sounds doesn't merely describe reality — they *create* coherence between energy and awareness. When you chant a Sanskrit mantra, you are not only speaking about the divine; you are resonating *as* the divine.

Each chakra resonates with a bīja mantra, or "seed sound." For Sahasrara, the sacred sound is OM (AUM) in its *transcendent form* — not as vibration, but as silence after sound.
OM begins with creation (*A*), sustains through existence (*U*), and dissolves into return (*M*). Yet in Sahasrara, we enter the stillness beyond even this — the fourth sound, *turīya*, the silence that is not absence but eternal presence.

When chanted, OM vibrates through the entire body: it begins in the chest, rises through the throat, illuminates the brow, and finally dissolves at the crown — where sound merges with light, and vibration becomes awareness. This moment of stillness is the gateway to transcendence, where all forms of separation fade into unity.

In the Sahasrara mandala, a thousand luminous petals radiate from a single center, each one a syllable of divine consciousness vibrating in harmony. Within this lotus lies a radiant point — the Bindu, the silent witness of all creation. Around it flows the eternal current of AUM, expanding into infinity and returning into peace.

Why does this matter today?
Because Sanskrit is not a language of the past — it is the resonance of the eternal now. Its mantras awaken dormant frequencies within your consciousness, realigning your being with the vibration of wholeness.

When you chant OM in devotion or in silence, you are not reciting sound —
you are remembering origin.
You are declaring:
I am light. I am awareness. I am one with the infinite.

OM at the Crown is not heard; it is *known.*
It does not echo through space; it radiates through being.
It does not end in silence — it becomes it.

Through Sahasrara, you awaken not to something new, but to what has always been true:
You are the eternal consciousness through which all light shines.

The Crown Chakra and Maslow's Hierarchy of Needs

In the mid-20th century, psychologist Abraham Maslow introduced his *Hierarchy of Needs* — a pyramid illustrating the progressive stages of human motivation, from physical survival to spiritual fulfillment. He proposed that once our basic needs are met, higher levels of awareness and purpose naturally awaken. At the pinnacle lies self-actualization, and beyond it, what Maslow later called self-transcendence — the recognition of unity, meaning, and connection with something greater than oneself.

Long before modern psychology, the ancient yogic tradition articulated this same principle through the chakra system. Each chakra represents a layer of consciousness — physical, emotional, mental, and spiritual — through which human awareness evolves. As each level is balanced and integrated, energy ascends, transforming instinct into intuition, and selfhood into soulhood.

The Crown Chakra, or Sahasrara, completes this evolutionary arc — uniting psychology and spirituality in a single truth: the fulfillment of all needs is found in the remembrance of our divine nature.

ROOT CHAKRA ↔ PHYSIOLOGICAL & SAFETY NEEDS

Muladhara corresponds to Maslow's foundational levels — the need for food, shelter, stability, and physical survival. It is the root of embodiment, teaching us to trust life and feel secure within existence itself. Without grounding, spiritual growth lacks foundation.

SACRAL CHAKRA ↔ BELONGING, PLEASURE & EMOTIONAL CONNECTION

Once safety is established, Svadhisthana awakens the desire for connection, intimacy, and creativity. It reflects the human longing to feel and to be felt — to experience joy, beauty, and emotional flow. When this center is balanced, relationships become expressions of harmony rather than dependency.

SOLAR PLEXUS CHAKRA ↔ ESTEEM, CONFIDENCE & SELF-MASTERY

In Manipura, self-awareness awakens as personal power. It corresponds to Maslow's esteem needs — achievement, independence, and confidence. This chakra ignites the will to act, to grow, and to direct one's destiny with integrity. Through its balance, purpose replaces control, and empowerment replaces domination.

HEART CHAKRA ↔ LOVE, COMPASSION & CONNECTION

Anahata bridges the human and the divine. It represents unconditional love, empathy, and forgiveness — needs that transcend survival or status. Through the heart, we begin to experience unity consciousness in human form, shifting from self-serving motivation to compassion and service.

THROAT CHAKRA ↔ AUTHENTIC EXPRESSION & SELF-ACTUALIZATION

Vishuddha governs truth, communication, and creativity. It reflects Maslow's level of self-actualization, where one expresses their authentic nature freely and aligns action with purpose. When energy flows here, the individual no longer imitates the world — they *inspire* it.

THIRD EYE CHAKRA ↔ INTUITION, INSIGHT & SELF-TRANSCENDENCE

Beyond self-actualization lies the realm of Ajna, the Third Eye Chakra — corresponding to Maslow's concept of self-transcendence. Here, perception moves beyond the personal mind into higher awareness. Intuition replaces analysis, and insight arises through silence. The self perceives its place within the greater pattern, seeing with the light of understanding rather than the lens of ego.

Ajna represents the dawning of meta-consciousness — the ability to observe thought without identification. It is where revelation begins and individuality begins to dissolve into the awareness of something eternal.

CROWN CHAKRA ↔ SELF-REALIZATION & DIVINE UNION

At the summit of both systems lies Sahasrara, the Crown Chakra — the point of *pure consciousness* and *spiritual unity.* Here, the journey through need and desire culminates in transcendence, not as escape, but as expansion.

In this stage, all lower needs are not denied but fulfilled through awareness. The hunger for love becomes oneness; the search for purpose becomes presence; the drive for achievement becomes devotion. The individual self merges into the universal field of being.

Where Ajna brings *insight*, Sahasrara brings *integration*. The mind that once sought meaning realizes it *is* meaning. This is the stage Maslow described in his later writings as the peak experience — a moment of unity, awe, and sacred belonging. Yet in Sahasrara, that moment becomes continuous — not a glimpse of transcendence, but life lived *as* transcendence.

Here, the pyramid of needs inverts: rather than climbing upward to reach fulfillment, we realize fulfillment flows downward — from Source into every level of being. The divine does not exist above life but *within it*, animating every breath, every cell, every thought with consciousness.

When Sahasrara awakens, motivation shifts from acquisition to awareness. We act not to gain, but to give. We love not to be loved, but because love is what we are. The Crown Chakra transforms existence from striving to serenity — the recognition that nothing is missing, and all is sacred.

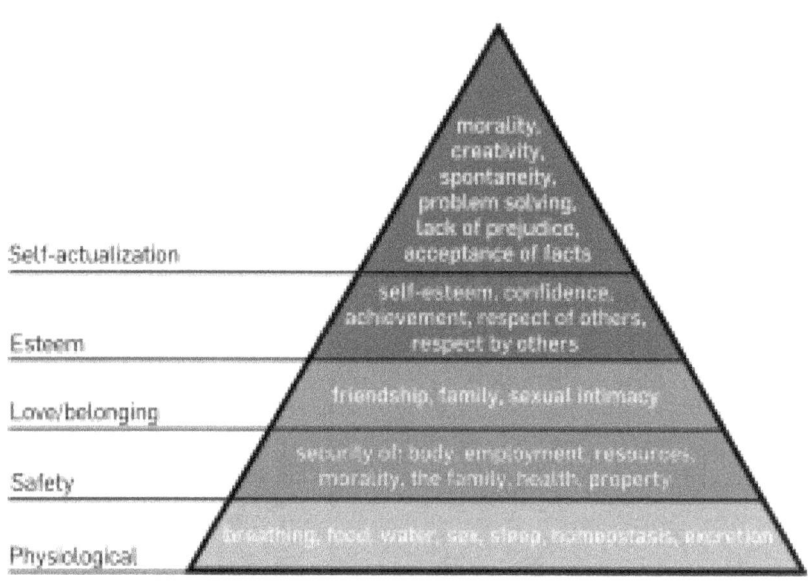

Mazlow's Hierarchy of Needs

Both Maslow's Hierarchy and the Chakra System describe the ascent of consciousness — from survival to surrender, from instinct to inspiration, from selfhood to Spirit.
Yet the highest truth of both is not found at the top, but at the center — in the realization that the same consciousness guiding our breath is the same consciousness moving galaxies.

When Sahasrara opens, the seeker becomes the sought.
The journey dissolves, and awareness rests in unity.

Fulfillment is no longer something to reach.
It is what you already are.

Crown Chakra ↔ Divine Consciousness, Enlightenment & Unity

The Crown Chakra (Sahasrara) is the seventh and highest energy center in the human system — the point where individual awareness merges with universal consciousness. Beyond perception and thought, Sahasrara represents *pure being* — the state where one no longer seeks connection, but realizes that connection has always existed.

Once perception awakens through the Third Eye, awareness transcends even vision itself. In the Crown, there is no longer a seeker and a source, a sound and a silence — only the presence that contains them both.

Sahasrara is the realm of divine remembrance — the awakening of consciousness to its own infinite nature.

DIVINE CONSCIOUSNESS: THE HUMAN DESIRE TO REMEMBER SOURCE

At its essence, the Crown Chakra governs the awareness of unity — the recognition that all life is woven from one field of consciousness. It teaches that enlightenment is not an achievement, but a realization: we are not becoming divine; we are remembering that we already are.

- Awareness Beyond Mind: When Sahasrara is open, the mind no longer controls awareness; awareness becomes the space in which thought arises and dissolves. It is the silence that witnesses all without judgment.
- Oneness of All Beings: The Crown expands empathy into unity. You no longer love others because you understand them — you love them because you *are* them. Separation fades, revealing an infinite field of interconnection.
- Stillness as Presence: True enlightenment is not the absence of thought, but the presence that remains when thought rests. Sahasrara reveals that peace is not found — it *is what remains* when seeking ends.
- Divine Intelligence: Through this center, we align with the intelligence that animates all existence. The universe ceases to be something outside us and becomes the consciousness looking through our own eyes.

ENLIGHTENMENT: THE BLOSSOMING OF THE THOUSAND-PETALED LOTUS

Sahasrara is symbolized by the thousand-petaled lotus, each petal representing a vibration of consciousness unfolding into infinity. When this lotus blooms, the soul experiences liberation — *moksha* — the freedom of knowing oneself as eternal.

- Union of Heaven and Earth: The Crown is both the summit and the source, where Spirit descends into form and form rises into Spirit. Here, divine energy flows downward as grace, integrating enlightenment into everyday life.

- Radiance of the Infinite: When the Crown is balanced, light radiates through the body like an inner sun. Joy becomes natural, wisdom effortless, and love unconditional.
- Surrender to the Whole: Enlightenment is not an escape from life but a surrender into it. Sahasrara teaches that the divine is not elsewhere — it breathes through every cell, every moment, every heartbeat.
- Silence as Truth: The highest mantra of the Crown is not sound, but silence — the stillness after OM. In that silence, consciousness recognizes itself as infinite awareness, beyond words or form.

UNITY: THE FUSION OF SELF AND SOURCE

Beyond the need to know lies the state of being known — the realization that consciousness and creation are one. The Crown Chakra embodies the union of self and Spirit, of the finite and the infinite.

- Wholeness in Existence: When Sahasrara is open, nothing feels missing. Every experience — joy, sorrow, birth, and death — is seen as an expression of divine order.
- Grace in Action: Unity consciousness transforms how we live. Compassion flows naturally, not as effort but as essence. Service becomes joy, and simplicity becomes wisdom.
- Beyond Belief: The Crown transcends doctrines and dogma. Truth becomes experiential, not conceptual — known through direct realization rather than inherited belief.
- The Return Home: Sahasrara is the final remembrance — the return to the source within. Enlightenment is not

a journey outward but a spiral inward, ending where it began: in the heart of divine awareness.

AUTHENTIC UNITY: THE ENERGY OF TRANSCENDENCE

The element of Sahasrara is beyond all elements — etheric light, the formless essence that gives rise to all matter. Its color, violet-white, symbolizes purity, divinity, and the blending of all frequencies into one radiant whole.

When balanced, the Crown Chakra allows energy to flow freely between the physical and spiritual realms, anchoring higher consciousness in human form.

- Embodied Spirit: Enlightenment is not leaving the body behind, but living in it as light. The awakened being walks the Earth yet vibrates with Heaven.
- Divine Flow: When the Crown is open, guidance flows effortlessly. Life aligns through synchronicity, intuition, and grace.
- Humble Illumination: True radiance carries no pride — it shines quietly, inspiring peace in others. The most enlightened are often the most ordinary, because they no longer need to be seen as special.
- Living Prayer: Every breath becomes devotion, every act a meditation. Through Sahasrara, being itself becomes a prayer — the soul's silent "yes" to existence.

WHY THIS MATTERS FOR ENERGY FLOW

The Crown Chakra is the fountainhead of energy in the human system. It receives divine consciousness and distributes it downward through every chakra, harmonizing the physical and spiritual bodies. When this channel is clear, enlightenment flows naturally — not as effort, but as grace.

If Sahasrara is weak or blocked:

- The Third Eye may become overactive, leading to confusion, detachment, or spiritual doubt. Insight without unity becomes fragmented.
- The Throat may lose inspiration, speaking truth without the resonance of higher wisdom.
- The Heart may struggle to hold unconditional love, mistaking empathy for obligation instead of expression of oneness.

When Sahasrara is balanced, every chakra below it glows in harmony. Energy moves freely from the divine source through the human vessel, completing the circuit of creation.

The Crown whispers:
"I am light. I am consciousness. I am one with all."

When Sahasrara awakens, the journey ends not in transcendence — but in presence.
We realize the destination was never elsewhere, because the divine has always been here — in this breath, this body, this boundless now.

Chapter 2 – Foundations of Sahasrara

Crown Chakra Basics: The Light Beyond All Form

If you are new to chakra study, the Crown Chakra, or Sahasrara, is the seventh and highest of the primary energy centers. It is located at the crown of the head, radiating upward like a halo of light, and energetically connects the physical body with the infinite field of consciousness.

Sahasrara is often called the *Thousand-Petaled Lotus* — symbolizing the full blossoming of human potential and the realization of divine unity. It governs the brain, nervous system, and pineal gland, linking biological intelligence with spiritual awareness. Whereas the Third Eye Chakra allows us to see truth, the Crown allows us to be truth — to experience consciousness not as something we reach, but as what we already are.

This chakra is the bridge between the human and the divine — the gateway through which awareness expands beyond individuality and merges with the source of all creation. Sahasrara is not about belief; it is about direct experience — the inner knowing that life itself is sacred, whole, and interconnected.

Its energy is subtle, luminous, and infinite — like white light refracting into every color of the spectrum. When balanced, the

Crown Chakra brings serenity, gratitude, and spiritual clarity. When blocked or closed, we may feel disconnected from meaning or Spirit, lost in intellectual analysis, or trapped in existential doubt.

When open, Sahasrara is not a concept to be understood but a state of consciousness to be lived — the effortless awareness that witnesses, loves, and creates through you.

KEY QUALITIES OF SAHASRARA

• Element: Beyond the Elements (Pure Consciousness) — transcending Earth, water, fire, air, and ether. Sahasrara is the field in which all elements arise and dissolve, representing infinite awareness and divine unity.

• Color: Violet to White Light — violet symbolizes transmutation and spiritual awakening, while pure white represents enlightenment and the blending of all frequencies into oneness.

• Symbol: A thousand-petaled lotus radiating white-violet light. At its center is a small circle of gold or luminous white, symbolizing the infinite nature of divine consciousness.

• Sound (Bīja Mantra): OM — in its silent aspect, representing the sound beyond sound, the vibration of universal creation and stillness.

• Location in the Body: Crown of the head, slightly above the scalp. The energy radiates upward and outward, connecting the human energy field with universal consciousness.

• Organs and Systems: Brain, nervous system, pineal and pituitary glands — the physical instruments of consciousness and spiritual perception.

• Core Themes: Enlightenment, unity, divine connection, transcendence, faith, awareness, bliss, surrender, and remembrance of Source.

THE LOTUS OF LIGHT

When Sahasrara is balanced, life feels radiant, purposeful, and divinely guided. You no longer feel separate from existence — you sense the pulse of creation within every breath. Joy arises without reason. Awareness expands beyond thought. Gratitude flows as a natural state of being.

When this chakra is blocked, one may feel spiritually adrift, skeptical, or numb to meaning. Disconnection from faith or higher guidance can manifest as depression, confusion, or mental exhaustion. Overactivity in the Crown Chakra can lead to escapism, ungrounded spirituality, or withdrawal from the physical world — a "floating" sense of detachment from reality.

The balance of Sahasrara is not found through effort but through surrender. When you let go of the need to control or understand, divine order reveals itself. The thousand-petaled lotus opens not through force but through trust.

AWAKENING THE CROWN

Sahasrara reminds us that enlightenment is not an ascent away from the human experience but the *illumination of it*. It is the awareness that the divine and the earthly are not separate — that the light of consciousness expresses itself through every heartbeat, every breath, every act of creation.

To balance or awaken the Crown Chakra:

• Meditate on Light: Visualize a radiant white or violet light above your head. With each breath, allow it to expand, surrounding your body in peace and stillness.

• Practice Gratitude: Gratitude opens the Crown. Acknowledge the beauty and order in all experiences, even the challenging ones. Gratitude transforms thought into prayer.
• Contemplate Unity: Reflect on the interconnectedness of all life. Notice how your breath, the trees, and the sky are part of one continuous rhythm.
• Chant OM in Silence: Begin by softly chanting OM, allowing the vibration to rise to the crown. Then fall into silence — listen for the soundless space that follows. That stillness is the voice of the divine.
• Ground the Light: Balance spiritual expansion with grounding practices — walking in nature, mindful breathing, or gentle movement. Enlightenment flourishes through embodiment.

When Sahasrara is clear, energy flows freely through every chakra below it — aligning body, mind, and Spirit into perfect coherence. Divine inspiration descends effortlessly, bringing peace, creativity, and wisdom into everyday life.

The Crown Chakra teaches that awakening is not about reaching higher realms but recognizing that the highest realm already exists within you.
When you rest in that awareness, there is nothing to seek — only everything to see.

You are the light, the lotus, and the silence from which all things arise.

Cross-Cultural Perspectives on the Crown Chakra

The concept of divine union — the realization that all life is interconnected and born of the same source — transcends all cultures, faiths, and philosophies.
Across civilizations, the Crown Chakra has been understood not

merely as an energy center, but as the sacred summit of consciousness — the bridge between the finite and the infinite.

Whether described as enlightenment, nirvana, Heaven, moksha, or the Great Spirit, the essence of Sahasrara remains universal: the awakening of consciousness to its own divine nature.

Where the Third Eye teaches us to see truth, the Crown allows us to *be* truth — to experience unity beyond perception, faith beyond belief, and love beyond form.

YOGIC TRADITION

In the yogic chakra system, Sahasrara (सहस्रार) means "thousand-petaled," symbolizing the infinite expansion of consciousness. It is depicted as a lotus of pure white or violet light, radiating from the crown of the head — the final unfolding of spiritual evolution.

Ancient yogic texts describe Sahasrara as the abode of pure awareness, where Shiva (consciousness) and Shakti (energy) merge in eternal union. This meeting represents liberation (*moksha*) — the realization that the seeker and the sought are one.

Unlike the lower chakras, Sahasrara has no specific element, for it transcends the material world entirely. It is beyond form, beyond duality, beyond even light and sound.
Here, the yogi experiences samadhi — the still point where the wave recognizes itself as the ocean.

When Sahasrara awakens, the individual ceases to act from ego or desire. Life unfolds through divine will, and the practitioner lives as an expression of consciousness itself — silent, radiant, and free.

BUDDHIST TRADITION

In Buddhism, the Crown Chakra aligns with the experience of enlightenment — the realization of *Bodhi*, or complete awakening. The thousand-petaled lotus mirrors the symbol of the Lotus Throne, upon which the Buddha sits — pure awareness blooming from the mud of human experience.

Sahasrara corresponds to the final stage of the Eightfold Path, where right understanding gives way to no-self (anatta) — the direct knowing that the self is not separate from the cosmos. When this awareness arises, suffering dissolves, and compassion becomes infinite.

Meditative practices such as Vipassana or Dzogchen guide practitioners toward this state of luminous emptiness — not a void, but a vast stillness filled with presence. In this silence, the universe breathes through the individual, and the individual breathes with the universe.

CHRISTIAN MYSTICISM

Within Christian mysticism, the Crown Chakra's essence resonates with the experience of divine union — the soul's merging with God through contemplation and surrender. Mystics such as Meister Eckhart, Teresa of Ávila, and John of the Cross spoke of this state as the "marriage of the soul and the divine."

The "crown of life" and "crown of glory" mentioned in the New Testament symbolize this same illumination — the reward not of achievement, but of awakening. The biblical phrase *"Be still and know that I am God"* reflects Sahasrara's core teaching: in stillness, one realizes that divinity is not external, but the essence of being itself.

For the Christian mystic, the light descending from Heaven is the same light that rises within — a reminder that grace flows both ways, from God to creation and from creation back to God.

INDIGENOUS AND SHAMANIC PERSPECTIVES

Among many Indigenous and shamanic cultures, the Crown represents the direct channel between the Earth and the Sky — the sacred axis connecting humanity to the Great Spirit. It is the point where prayers ascend and blessings descend.

In Native American, First Nations, and Andean teachings, the human being is viewed as the bridge between the physical and spiritual worlds — rooted in the Earth through the Root Chakra, and open to the heavens through the Crown.

Ceremonies of communion with the ancestors, sun rituals, and celestial dances all echo the activation of Sahasrara — where consciousness expands beyond the self to embrace all existence. In these traditions, enlightenment is not separation from the world but *oneness with it* — the awareness that the Creator lives through every form, every breath, every heartbeat.

TAOIST AND EAST ASIAN PHILOSOPHY

In Taoist teachings, the Crown corresponds to the Niwan Palace or "Mud Pill Palace," the highest spiritual center in the head where Heaven's energy (*Tian Qi*) enters the human form. It represents the return to Wu Wei — effortless harmony with the Tao.

Just as the yogic Sahasrara unites Shiva and Shakti, Taoist alchemy seeks the union of Heaven (Yang) and Earth (Yin) within the body. When balanced, this union restores the original state of the *immortal Spirit* — consciousness in harmony with the Way.

In Chinese calligraphy, the character for "enlightenment" (悟, *wu*) depicts the heart and mind as one — a perfect reflection of the Crown's teaching that true wisdom arises when intellect surrenders to awareness.

MYSTICAL AND RELIGIOUS SYMBOLISM

Across the world's traditions, the Crown has been depicted as a radiant symbol of divine consciousness:

• In Hinduism, it is the Sahasrara Padma — the lotus where divine union is achieved.
• In Buddhism, it is the Thousand-Petaled Lotus of Enlightenment — the full awakening of the Buddha nature.
• In Christian mysticism, it becomes the Halo — the golden light of divine illumination surrounding saints and angels.
• In Judaism, it aligns with the Keter Sephirah in the Kabbalistic Tree of Life — the crown of divine will and the source of creation.
• In Islamic Sufism, it is mirrored in Fana, the annihilation of the self in God, where only the Beloved remains.
• In Egyptian spirituality, the golden disk above the head of Ra and Hathor symbolizes the same divine illumination — the solar crown of eternal life.

Across all cultures, the message remains eternal:
The highest form of knowledge is unity — the remembrance that consciousness is one, expressed through many.

THE UNIVERSAL TEACHING

Though names differ — Sahasrara, Keter, Nirvana, Moksha, Heaven, or The Great Spirit — every path points toward the same realization: that divinity is not something to reach, but something to remember.

The Crown Chakra is the silent summit where all paths converge — where science meets Spirit, East meets West, and seeker meets self.

When the thousand-petaled lotus blooms, there is no longer religion or philosophy, form or formlessness. There is only awareness — vast, luminous, and whole.

To awaken Sahasrara is to return home to the consciousness that has never left.

It is not about rising above the world, but realizing that you are the world —
and the world is divine.

LIGHT AND DIVINE UNITY DEITIES

Across world mythologies, gods and goddesses of light, sky, and transcendence embody the essence of the Crown Chakra (Sahasrara) — the thousand-petaled lotus of divine consciousness.
Their symbols — radiant crowns, halos, ascending rays, and celestial fires — represent the culmination of awakening: *not merely to see light, but to become it.*

While Ajna governs the *illumination of vision*, Sahasrara represents the *dissolution of vision into pure awareness.*
The deities of this realm do not reveal truth — they *are* truth.
They do not seek divinity — they *emanate* it.

Across traditions, the message remains eternal:
Light is not a thing we perceive. Light is what we are.

HINDUISM

In yogic and Tantric cosmology, Sahasrara is the abode of *pure consciousness* — the union of Shiva (pure awareness) and Shakti (divine energy).
Here, the seeker realizes that the dance of creation and dissolution arises within the same infinite stillness.

Shiva, the supreme consciousness, is often depicted with a crescent moon above his head — symbolizing transcendence beyond the cycles of time. When Kundalini Shakti ascends through all the chakras and unites with Shiva at the crown, *samadhi* (liberation) occurs.

The goddess Saraswati, born of Brahma's creative word, represents the flow of divine wisdom through sound, art, and knowledge — the descent of higher consciousness into human understanding.
Meanwhile, Brahman, the Absolute, remains beyond all form — the eternal presence that Sahasrara reveals within every being.

BUDDHISM

In Buddhism, the Crown Chakra corresponds to the *Thousand-Petaled Lotus of Enlightenment* — the complete flowering of consciousness. The Buddha's radiant crown symbolizes *Bodhi*, the state of awakening in which self and cosmos dissolve into one luminous field.

The Dharmakaya, or "Body of Truth," represents the same infinite awareness as Sahasrara — formless, boundless, and eternal. The golden halo surrounding depictions of the Buddha mirrors the aura of enlightenment, radiating compassion and wisdom in all directions.

Deities such as Vairocana, the Cosmic Buddha, embody this universal consciousness — the light from which all Buddhas arise. Vairocana's name itself means "He Who Shines Everywhere," reflecting the all-pervading brilliance of awakened mind.

CHRISTIAN MYSTICISM

In Christian iconography, the halo — a radiant circle of gold or white — signifies divine illumination and the realization of union with God.
Saints, angels, and Christ himself are shown crowned with light, representing the transfiguration of human nature into divine presence.

Christ's words, *"I and the Father are one,"* encapsulate Sahasrara's essence — the awareness that separation is illusion and that divine consciousness is our true identity.
The "Crown of Glory" and "Crown of Life" spoken of in Scripture symbolize this inner awakening — not a reward for effort, but the realization of grace.

The mystics of Christianity — Teresa of Ávila, Meister Eckhart, and St. John of the Cross — all described the same ascent: the soul's final surrender into the silence where self and God become one. In this union, prayer dissolves into presence, and the seeker becomes the light they once sought.

EGYPTIAN TRADITION

In ancient Egypt, Ra, the sun god, wore the *solar disk* as his crown — the eternal light of divine order and renewal.
This solar crown mirrors the radiant halo of Sahasrara, symbolizing the eternal cycle of life, death, and rebirth as expressions of one infinite source.

Hathor, goddess of beauty and cosmic harmony, is often shown with a crown of solar light cradled between cow horns — representing the fusion of Heaven and Earth, form and Spirit.

Thoth, the god of wisdom and divine language, bridges human understanding and cosmic mind — the mediator through whom light becomes law.

For the Egyptians, enlightenment was not escape from the world but *alignment* with Ma'at — the divine order that binds creation in balance and truth.
Sahasrara represents this same cosmic equilibrium — the awareness that all things unfold within the light of consciousness.

GREEK AND ROMAN MYSTICISM

In Greek thought, Apollo, god of the sun and music, personifies illumination in both mind and cosmos. His light is not only physical but intellectual — the clarity of divine understanding. The laurel crown he wears represents victory over ignorance, much like the lotus crown of Sahasrara represents freedom from illusion.

Zeus and Helios both embody the radiant force of Heaven — energy descending as lightning or sunlight, awakening creation. The philosopher Plotinus, inspired by the Mysteries, described the final stage of enlightenment as the "Flight of the Alone to the Alone" — an exact expression of the Crown Chakra's transcendence beyond individuality.

INDIGENOUS AND SHAMANIC COSMOLOGIES

For many Indigenous and shamanic traditions, the Crown represents the sky world — the realm of the ancestors, stars, and celestial beings.
The Sun Spirit or Sky Father embodies the consciousness of the heavens, while the Earth Mother holds the life force below. The shaman, standing between them, is the bridge of light — much like the awakened Sahasrara connecting human awareness with the infinite.

Rituals of sunrise prayer, celestial song, and smoke offerings to the Great Spirit reflect the human recognition of divine unity. Just as Sahasrara channels cosmic light into form, the shaman channels vision into wisdom — bringing Heaven to Earth through sacred presence.

KABBALISTIC AND SUFI MYSTICISM

In Kabbalah, Sahasrara aligns with the sefirah Keter, meaning "Crown." It is the highest emanation of the Tree of Life — pure divine will and the spark of creation itself. Keter is the ineffable source from which all other aspects of existence flow, representing infinite compassion and unity.

In Sufism, the Crown corresponds to Fana, the annihilation of the self in God. The Sufi mystic's cry, *"Ana al-Haqq"* ("I am the Truth"), echoes the realization of Sahasrara — the merging of human awareness with divine essence.
The *whirling dervish*, spinning in harmony with creation, mirrors the thousand-petaled lotus in motion — the dance of consciousness around the still center of oneness.

LIGHT-BASED SPIRITUALITY

From the sacred fires of Zoroastrian temples to the candles of Christian altars, from Buddhist butter lamps to Hindu Diwali lights, humanity has always turned to flame as a symbol of divine presence.

If Ajna's light *reveals*, Sahasrara's light *dissolves*. It is not illumination of the mind but illumination of *being*.

Practices of divine light appear across traditions:

• Hindu Sahasrara meditation — visualizing the thousand-petaled lotus opening to receive the cosmic current.
• Buddhist Clear Light practice — resting in the luminous void

beyond form and thought.
• Christian contemplative prayer — merging into the "Uncreated Light" of God's presence.
• Sufi remembrance (dhikr) — invoking the Divine Name until only the vibration of unity remains.
• Indigenous sun ceremonies — greeting the dawn as rebirth, the renewal of sacred light within and without.

Each path honors the same truth: that the flame we light is not to dispel darkness, but to recognize that light has never been absent.

ORIGINS AND SACRED HISTORY OF SAHASRARA

The earliest references to Sahasrara appear in the Tantras and the Shat-Chakra-Nirupana, where it is described as the lotus of infinite petals, radiant with eternal light. Unlike the lower chakras, it is not a center *within* the body but a *gateway beyond* it — the aperture through which consciousness expands into the cosmos.

In yogic symbolism, the upward-pointing energy of Kundalini rises from the Root to unite with Paramashiva at the Crown. This meeting is not a mystical event, but the realization that they were never separate — that energy and awareness, matter and Spirit, always existed as one.

Ancient Vedic seers described this realization as Sat-Chit-Ananda — Being, Consciousness, Bliss — the direct experience of existence as divine.

In this state, there is no perceiver or perceived, only pure presence.
The thousand-petaled lotus blooms, not as a symbol of ascent, but as the unfolding of eternity within the heart of now.

Across all cultures — from the solar crowns of Egypt to the halos of Christ, from the lotus of the Buddha to the Keter of Kabbalah — humanity has celebrated the same revelation:

The divine light that crowns the heavens also dwells within.

To awaken the Crown Chakra is to realize the ultimate simplicity — that we are not reaching for God, we are remembering that we were never apart.

When Sahasrara opens, life becomes the prayer, and light becomes the self.
Not a light that shines, but a light that *is*.

THE SYMBOLISM OF THE CROWN CHAKRA

The Crown Chakra (Sahasrara) is the final gateway — the thousand-petaled lotus where consciousness blossoms into infinity.
Unlike the other chakras, it is *beyond element, beyond form, beyond color as we know it.* It represents the pure field of awareness — light so refined that it ceases to be light *seen* and becomes light *being.*

Sahasrara is not about perception, but presence. It is the point where the seeker dissolves into the sought, where the journey of ascent ends in the eternal return to Source.
If Ajna reveals truth, Sahasrara *is* truth — the awareness behind all revelation, the silence that contains all sound, the stillness that holds all motion.

Its symbol is the thousand-petaled lotus, radiant in white and violet hues, representing the infinite unfoldment of consciousness. Each petal is a vibration of realization — an aspect of awakening blooming from the center of divine unity. The lotus does not open outward to seek the sun; it *is* the sun — the light through which all things are seen.

At the heart of Sahasrara rests the bindu — a luminous point of pure awareness. It is the origin and the return, the unmanifest from which manifestation flows. In this single point, all opposites converge: self and Spirit, time and eternity, sound and silence.

While Ajna governs the light of perception, Sahasrara embodies the light of realization — awareness without object, illumination without limit.
It is not the eye that sees, but the consciousness that knows itself as everything seen.

Sahasrara teaches us that enlightenment is not a destination reached through effort, but the remembrance of what has always been true:
We are the light — eternal, infinite, divine.

THE THOUSAND-PETALED LOTUS

The lotus of Sahasrara is unlike any other in the chakra system. Where the lower lotuses represent specific energies or qualities of experience, this one symbolizes infinite potential — the totality of being awakened to itself.

Depicted as a radiant blossom with a thousand luminous petals (a poetic symbol for infinity), its color shifts from violet to white, merging all frequencies of the spectrum into one field of divine radiance.

Violet represents spiritual transmutation — the alchemy of the soul returning to light.

White symbolizes unity — the presence of all colors dissolved into pure illumination.

The thousand petals are said to correspond to countless states of realization — each an awakening within awakening, each revealing another layer of wholeness.

This is consciousness in full bloom: awareness unfolding from the center outward, then returning from the outer world back to the source within.

The thousand-petaled lotus opens only through surrender — not through striving or control, but through stillness, humility, and grace.

It blossoms when the mind becomes transparent enough for divine light to pass through unhindered.

It opens when love becomes the only language, and silence becomes the only prayer.

Within the lotus lies a small circle of golden light — the bindu, the seed of consciousness. It represents the eternal truth that every being carries the whole within.

When Sahasrara awakens, the circle of the self expands to include the cosmos, and the universe itself becomes the meditation.

To contemplate the Crown Chakra is to gaze into infinity — not above, but within.

It reminds us that enlightenment is not rising above the world but *seeing the divine in everything within it.*

THE COLOR WHITE AND VIOLET OF SAHASRARA

While the lower chakras each vibrate within distinct frequencies of the visible spectrum, Sahasrara transcends them all.
Its hues are the highest frequencies of light — violet and white — representing the synthesis of every color, every vibration, every possibility.

White is the color of unity — all wavelengths combined in perfect harmony. It is the light of total awareness, where nothing is separate, and all opposites resolve into wholeness. Violet, the final visible color before light becomes ultraviolet and invisible, symbolizes the threshold between form and formlessness, time and eternity, self and Source.

Together, these colors express transcendence through inclusion: the realization that enlightenment is not rejection of the world but the understanding that everything — from root to crown — is divine.

WHITE: THE LIGHT OF UNITY

White is the color of absolute awareness — not a light that shines upon things, but the light *from which* all things shine. It is consciousness before it takes on color or form — the original radiance underlying creation.

When the Crown Chakra is open, this white light fills the energy field, dissolving tension and illusion. It is the awareness that purifies, heals, and integrates all aspects of the self. This is the "light of grace" spoken of by mystics — not something earned, but something *remembered*.

White light carries the vibration of stillness — the silence after OM, the peace beyond understanding. It holds all sounds, all colors, all experiences within one infinite presence.

To meditate on white light is to rest in the essence of being —
not visualizing, but allowing yourself to *become* the light that
observes.

VIOLET: THE LIGHT OF TRANSMUTATION

Violet bridges the seen and unseen — the final color before
human perception dissolves into invisible frequencies. It is the
color of transformation, representing the alchemy of Spirit,
where the finite dissolves into the infinite.

Violet refines every vibration beneath it, transmuting density
into radiance, thought into awareness, and personality into
presence.
It is the frequency of surrender — of letting go into divine will,
where individual striving melts into flow.

When Sahasrara radiates violet light, the soul recognizes itself
as part of a vast cosmic intelligence — both the spark and the
flame, both drop and ocean.

Violet is the hue of faith — the willingness to trust the unseen,
to rest in mystery, to allow consciousness to unfold itself
without interference.

In this vibration, enlightenment becomes simple.
It is no longer an experience to chase, but a homecoming to the
presence that never left.

THE FREQUENCY OF ENLIGHTENMENT

White and violet together form the harmonic frequency of
Sahasrara — the octave of divine remembrance.
They symbolize the culmination of the soul's ascent from
matter to Spirit, from survival to surrender, from separation to
unity.

When the Crown Chakra vibrates in balance, all other chakras align naturally. Energy flows as one continuous current — love descending, light ascending — the dance of creation fulfilled within consciousness itself.

At this frequency, life becomes meditation. Every breath is prayer, every act a reflection of the divine.
You no longer search for meaning; *you are meaning embodied.*
You no longer seek light; *you are the light realizing itself through form.*

WHY WHITE AND VIOLET BELONG TO THE CROWN CHAKRA

Each chakra color reflects a state of consciousness, a phase in the soul's unfolding from Earth to ether. White and violet, the highest vibrations in the visible spectrum, correspond to Sahasrara, the crown of divine awareness.

Where indigo (Ajna) reveals insight and understanding, violet and white dissolve the very distinction between seer and seen. They represent *total integration* — the awareness in which all dualities merge and dissolve.

• Violet refines perception into realization — the awareness that transforms understanding into liberation.
• White unifies all frequencies — the state of wholeness in which the soul remembers its source.

In the visible rainbow, violet is the final hue before light becomes invisible — just as Sahasrara is the final chakra before consciousness transcends individuality.
White, the union of all colors, reflects the same truth in reverse — the return of multiplicity into one.

Together, they express the rhythm of the cosmos: expansion and return, creation and completion, light becoming life and life returning to light.

To meditate upon the violet-white radiance of Sahasrara is to enter the eternal circle of consciousness itself — the infinite stillness where awareness rests as both the dream and the dreamer, both the light and the one who sees.

When the thousand-petaled lotus opens, there is no above or below, no inner or outer.
There is only light — silent, whole, eternal.
This is Sahasrara — the Crown of Consciousness, the light that contains all lights.

VIOLET & WHITE IN DAILY LIFE

• When you feel disconnected from higher guidance or divine purpose:
Wear violet, white, or golden-hued clothing, scarves, or jewelry to attune to Sahasrara's frequency of light and unity.
Violet refines thought into spiritual clarity, while white expands awareness into peace. These colors open the Crown Chakra, quieting mental striving and reconnecting you to the divine intelligence that flows through all life.
They remind you that you are guided — not by will, but by wisdom.

• When the Spirit feels heavy or the mind restless:
Close your eyes and visualize breathing in white-violet light — soft, radiant, and weightless, descending from above your head like a waterfall of illumination.
Let it fill your crown, your mind, your heart, and your entire being.
Feel it dissolving tension, doubt, and resistance — replacing them with serenity, openness, and grace.

This light reminds you that surrender is not defeat; it is the soul returning home to peace.

• When seeking divine connection or higher consciousness:
Hold or wear crystals aligned with Sahasrara's frequency, such as amethyst, selenite, clear quartz, or lepidolite.
These stones act as conduits for pure energy, calming the nervous system and amplifying meditative states.
During prayer or reflection, place a crystal above the crown of your head or hold it gently in your palms.
Let its vibration lift your awareness beyond thought, opening the channel between your human mind and divine consciousness.
The goal is not to ascend — but to *remember* that you were never separate from the light.

• In rituals of transcendence and grace:
Light white or violet candles to symbolize spiritual illumination.
Burn sacred resins like frankincense, lotus, or lavender to elevate the atmosphere and purify the aura.
Meditate beneath open sky, at dawn or dusk, when Heaven and Earth touch in still light.
Surround yourself with soft fabrics, radiant tones, and sacred geometry that evoke purity and peace — circles, halos, or lotus patterns.
Let silence be your offering, for in silence the infinite reveals itself.

Violet and white in daily life remind you to rise beyond duality, to live as both soul and human, heaven and earth in harmony.
When you invite these colors into your awareness, you open to divine inspiration, faith, and unity — not as concepts, but as living truths within you.
To dwell in the light of Sahasrara is to *be* the blessing — to walk through the world as a vessel of peace, radiance, and grace.

MEDITATION WITH WHITE-VIOLET LIGHT

1. Sit comfortably, spine straight, and bring awareness to the crown of your head — the space where heaven meets your human form.
2. Visualize a thousand-petaled lotus unfolding slowly, each petal shimmering with violet and white light.
3. With each inhale, imagine divine light descending into the lotus; with each exhale, feel it radiating through your entire being.
4. Allow this light to fill your mind, dissolve boundaries, and expand awareness into stillness.
5. Silently repeat:
   "I am light. I am peace. I am one with all that is."

Remain in this glow for as long as you wish. The meditation ends not by closing the lotus, but by realizing that it was never closed — that you are forever connected to Source.

WANT TO EXPERIENCE IT IN ACTION?...
Watch this video for the Third Eye Chakra Meditation.
Watch it here: https://youtu.be/Fi5gfmnOrhs

THE DEEPER LESSON OF VIOLET AND WHITE

Violet and white teach that enlightenment is not about escaping life, but embracing it as light in motion.
They remind us that the divine does not dwell elsewhere — it breathes through every thought, every heartbeat, every moment of awareness.

Violet whispers: *"Transform what you touch into light."*
White answers: *"There is only light."*

Together, they reveal that consciousness and creation are not two — they are the same eternal radiance experienced from different sides of the veil.

Sahasrara's energy is the culmination of all the chakras — every insight, every emotion, every prayer returning to the silence from which it was born.
It teaches that to live spiritually is not to reach upward, but to open inward — to realize that divinity has always been at the center of your being.

When you live in the frequency of white-violet light, you no longer seek miracles — you become one.
Peace flows not from control, but from communion.
You see the world not as separate from you, but as light expressing itself through countless forms.

To awaken the Crown Chakra is to live in remembrance:
You are the prayer, the light, and the peace you have been searching for.

The Thousand-Petaled Lotus Of Sahasrara

At the summit of the human energy system blooms the thousand-petaled lotus of Sahasrara — the Crown Chakra — radiant with light beyond color, sound beyond vibration, and consciousness beyond thought.
It is not a chakra in the ordinary sense, for it transcends element, form, and individuality. It is the flowering of awareness into infinity — the realization that the seeker, the seeking, and the sought are one.

Where Ajna's two-petaled lotus reconciles duality, Sahasrara's thousand-petaled lotus dissolves it completely.
Here, polarity finds rest in unity, and all movement returns to stillness.
This lotus does not open through effort or concentration but through surrender — through the quiet remembrance that enlightenment is not attained, but revealed when resistance ends.

Sahasrara's lotus is described as pure white or radiant violet — light that contains all other colors, consciousness that includes all other states.

Each of its thousand petals symbolizes the infinite dimensions of realization — awareness unfolding and refolding upon itself in eternal cycles of creation and return.

Every petal is a revelation, a frequency of awakening, a note in the cosmic symphony of being.

The thousand-petaled lotus is not reached by climbing; it opens by *remembering*.

Its roots rest in the heart, its stem rises through the spine, and its blossom crowns the head — the bridge between heaven and earth.

It teaches that enlightenment is not an ascent from the body, but the illumination of the body by the light of Spirit.

THE SEED SOUND OF SAHASRARA

Unlike other chakras, Sahasrara has no single seed syllable — for it vibrates beyond vibration, resonating with the silent frequency of pure being.

Yet, in many traditions, the sacred sound OM (ॐ) or its extended form AUM is contemplated here as the eternal resonance of the cosmos.

- A represents creation — the awakening of awareness.
- U represents preservation — the continuity of consciousness.
- M represents dissolution — the return of all form into formlessness.
  And the silence following the chant represents the infinite stillness of Sahasrara — the soundless sound from which all sounds arise.

This silence is not absence but total presence.
It is the resting of the universe within itself — the hum of

eternity beyond all syllables.

To meditate on this sound is to become aware of the awareness that hears it — the witness before sound and after silence.

THE QUALITIES OF DIVINE CONSCIOUSNESS

The thousand petals of Sahasrara unfold as the flowering of divine qualities — aspects of the soul realized through union with Source.

Each petal represents a luminous truth of being:

- Unity: The realization that there is no separation between self and cosmos.
- Grace: The effortless unfolding of life as divine intelligence.
- Peace: The stillness beneath all change, the calm of infinite awareness.
- Wisdom: Knowledge beyond thought, insight born of presence.
- Love: The radiant field that sustains all creation, boundless and unconditional.
- Bliss: The joy of consciousness knowing itself as infinite.

When the Crown Chakra awakens, these qualities are not cultivated — they simply are.

They emanate naturally, like fragrance from a flower that has bloomed.

THE GEOMETRY OF INFINITY

The sacred geometry of Sahasrara transcends the limited forms of triangles and circles. It is the mandala of light — concentric, infinite, and self-illuminating.

At its center lies the bindu — the point of pure awareness from which the universe emanates and to which it returns.

If Ajna's circle and triangle represent perception becoming wisdom, Sahasrara's mandala represents wisdom dissolving into pure being.
It is the completion of the spiritual spiral — the end of separation, the return to origin.

Within this geometry, the thousand petals radiate like cosmic rays — each a beam of consciousness reflecting a different aspect of the One.
They are not separate; they are simultaneous expressions of the infinite.
Just as a prism breaks white light into color, Sahasrara gathers all color back into light.

THE TWO FLOWS OF ENERGY

Within the awakening of the Crown, two great streams of energy converge — Shiva (pure awareness) descending as light and Shakti (creative energy) ascending as life.
Their meeting at the crown is the sacred marriage — the moment of realization that the dancer and the dance have never been apart.

- The Descending Current (Shiva): Consciousness flowing downward, blessing matter with awareness.
- The Ascending Current (Shakti): Energy rising upward, returning experience to source.

When they unite, the circuit is complete — heaven and earth are joined, spirit and matter become one continuum.
This is enlightenment not as escape, but as integration — the world illumined by consciousness, and consciousness expressed through the world.

THE SACRED NUMBER ONE THOUSAND

In mystical numerology, one thousand does not signify a literal count but the innumerable — the infinite expansions of consciousness without limit.
It represents *completion through multiplicity*, the realization that all forms are expressions of the same essence.

Where the number two (Ajna) symbolized duality reconciled, one thousand represents unity infinitely expressed — the One appearing as the many, the many returning to the One.

Every petal of Sahasrara is a doorway through which awareness experiences itself anew — creation breathing, expanding, contracting, and dissolving in endless rhythm.

THE LOTUS AND THE COSMIC RAIN

In ancient yogic texts, the thousand-petaled lotus is said to shower Amrita, the nectar of immortality, upon the awakened being.
This nectar flows down through all chakras, bathing them in divine grace and restoring perfect balance.
It is not a substance but a frequency — the sweetness of pure awareness permeating body and mind.

In this flow, the physical body becomes luminous, thoughts become transparent, and emotions become radiant expressions of love.
The being lives not as an individual self but as a channel of divine presence — consciousness in motion, peace in form.

THE SYMBOLISM OF SAHASRARA IN THE TAROT

In the language of symbols, Sahasrara's energy appears wherever completion, illumination, and unity are depicted.

The Major Arcana:

- The Star (XVII): The descent of divine grace — light pouring from the heavens into the waters of creation.
- The Sun (XIX): Consciousness realized — radiant joy, wholeness, and clarity.
- Judgment (XX): Awakening from separation — the trumpet call of Spirit recalling the soul to light.
- The World (XXI): Completion and cosmic unity — the dancer within the mandala, embodying heaven and earth in perfect balance.

These cards echo Sahasrara's teaching: that enlightenment is not an end but a return to wholeness — life seen through the eyes of divinity.

THE WHITE LOTUS OF DIVINE UNION

The thousand-petaled lotus is sometimes depicted as white with a golden center — the White Lotus of Brahman, the flower of divine union.
Its whiteness signifies the total spectrum of light unified in one radiance.
Its golden heart symbolizes the eternal flame of consciousness — the sun within the crown.

When meditated upon, this lotus radiates peace that transcends understanding.
It teaches that awakening is not the annihilation of individuality but its illumination — the realization that every soul is a spark of the same eternal fire.

To live from Sahasrara is to see with the eyes of the Infinite —
to recognize that everything you touch, see, or breathe is God
meeting itself.

THE CIRCLE OF RETURN

Ajna's geometry of two resolves into Sahasrara's geometry of
one — the full circle of consciousness.
Vision becomes knowing, knowing becomes being.
The witness dissolves into the witnessed, and light remembers
itself as the source.

The thousand-petaled lotus is not somewhere above your head;
it is the true nature of awareness within you — infinite, silent,
and eternal.
When it opens, heaven and earth are no longer separate realms
but one vast field of consciousness, endlessly expressing itself
through the dance of existence.

To meditate upon the thousand-petaled lotus is to let yourself
dissolve into peace.
It is to know — not think, not believe, but *know* — that
everything is light, and that you are that light.

When Sahasrara blooms, there is no more striving for vision or
wisdom.
There is only being.
Only love.
Only the radiant stillness of the infinite awakening to itself.

SAHASRARA IN YOGIC PRACTICE

In the earliest Tantric and yogic teachings, the chakras are
luminous centers of consciousness—gateways where divine
awareness expresses through human form. Each center opens a
distinct octave of realization.
Sahasrara, the Crown Chakra, is the culmination of this ascent:

the flowering of consciousness into oneness—where individuality relaxes into the light of the Absolute.

The Sanskrit word Sahasrara (सहस्रार) means "thousand-petaled," pointing to infinite expansion. It is not a chakra of element or effort, but of *remembering*.
Where Ajna refines perception into wisdom, Sahasrara dissolves wisdom into pure being.

There is no fixed element here—Sahasrara is *beyond* the tattvas (earth, water, fire, air, ether). Its "element" is pure consciousness.
The traditional bīja for this summit is paradoxical: OM—and beyond OM, silence. OM points to creation, preservation, and dissolution; the silence after OM (turīya) reveals the Presence before and beyond all sound.

In practice, the Crown opens through surrender more than striving: devotion, deep meditation, humble service, and grace. Just as Vishuddha purifies through sound and Ajna illumines through vision, Sahasrara sanctifies through Presence—the effortless awareness in which all arises and subsides.

Yogic adepts regard the Crown as the aperture of liberation (brahmarandhra)—the meeting of ascending Shakti (life-force) with descending Shiva (pure awareness). When these currents unite, separation softens and the practitioner abides in samādhi—rest as the Self.

Traditional approaches that ripen the Crown include:

- Nididhyāsana (abidance in the Self): resting awareness in awareness.
- Śāmbhavī mudrā (practiced softly, after Ajna is stable): awareness lifted through the crown into vast space.
- Japa & contemplative prayer: the Name dissolving into namelessness.

- Seva (selfless service): ego thins; love shines.
- Yoga Nidra / deep stillness: the body sleeps while awareness remains awake.

The Crown is not *achieved*. It reveals itself when effort grows quiet.
When Sahasrara awakens, life is seen as one unbroken field of light—thoughts, bodies, seasons, stars, all shimmering in the same awareness.

THE INNER SYMBOL OF SAHASRARA

At the summit blooms the thousand-petaled lotus, radiant in violet-white.

- The petals signify innumerable realizations—consciousness awakening to itself again and again.
- At the center rests the bindu, a point of pure light—the source and return of all experience.
- Around the bindu, the subtle glow of OM may be contemplated—yet the symbol ultimately invites the silence beyond OM.

This mandala teaches: Being is the mantra.
When the mind grows transparent, love, wisdom, and peace arise without effort.
The geometry of Sahasrara is the circle of infinity—no edges, no opposite. Here, awareness does not look at light; it is light.

WHAT OM (AND SILENCE) REPRESENTS AT THE CROWN

• The Primordial Continuum
OM vibrates as A-U-M—creation, sustenance, dissolution. The fourth is the soundless: *turīya*, the ground of Being. At Sahasrara, we honor OM and rest in the hush that remains, recognizing awareness as the true "listener."

• Light Returning to Source
Where Ajna feels OM in the brow and skull, Sahasrara diffuses
it into space above the head. The vibration thins into presence—
like dawn brightening into day until no single ray can be found.

• Bridge of Union
OM here is not a tool to reach the divine, but a reminder that the
divine is our nature. Chanting becomes beholding; sound yields
to Being.

THE "SEED SOUND" OF SAHASRARA

Strictly, Sahasrara has no single bīja.
Traditions invite contemplation of OM, So'ham ("I am That"),
or Silence itself.

- OM attunes the field to the cosmic rhythm.
- So'ham dissolves "I" into "That," stabilizing unity.
- Silence (māuna) unveils the Self already present.

Choose one with reverence—then allow it to resolve into quiet.

THE POWER OF OM (AS IT FLOWERS INTO SILENCE)

• From Effort to Ease
Let the A rise from the belly, the U glide through heart and
throat, the M hum in skull and crown—then do not continue.
Rest in the after-sound. This is the doorway.

• Purifying the Crown Channel
Sahasrara may be veiled by existential doubt, over-
intellectualizing, or spiritual bypass. OM steadies faith; the
silence after OM exposes subtle grasping and invites release.

• Embodied Unity
At the Crown, realization is not escape but infusion. Insight

descends as compassion; peace becomes action; love becomes
service.

THE MYSTERY OF OM

The Māṇḍūkya Upaniṣad proclaims: *"OM is all this."*
At the Crown, the teaching ripens: the silence after OM is also
all this.
It is the unmistakable intimacy of awareness with itself—closer
than breath, wider than sky.

CHANTING OM / RESTING IN SILENCE

Chant to polish the lens; silence to realize the light.

Step 1 — Prepare

- Sit tall, crown gently lifted.
- Relax jaw, scalp, and the space above the head.
- Feel the breath arrive from "everywhere."

Step 2 — Attune

- Visualize a violet-white lotus opening above the crown.
- Sense a cool, radiant hush pervading the room.

Step 3 — Chant

- Exhale: A—U—M (3–7 times).
- Let the final M feather into a whisper of stillness at the
  crown.

Step 4 — Abide

- Drop the sound.
- Rest as aware silence—not doing stillness, being it.

Step 5 — Return with Grace

- Bring a palm to heart, one to crown.
- Whisper inwardly: *"I am That."*
- Open your eyes softly, carrying the quiet with you.

WAYS TO PRACTICE IN DAILY LIFE

- Morning Remembrance: 3 gentle OMs, then 3 minutes in silence. Let quiet set the day's rhythm.
- Before Service or Work: Touch crown lightly; breathe "So" in, "ham" out—2 minutes. Act from unity, not urgency.
- When Doubt Arises: Place awareness above the head; feel the "open sky." Whisper *"Let it be Light."*
- Walking as Prayer: With each step: *"I am"* (step), *"That"* (step). Let the body move in God.
- Group Practice: End circles with one OM, then shared silence. Notice how the room itself "glows."

LIGHT-CENTERED AFFIRMATION FOR SAHASRARA

"As silence follows OM, peace follows me.
I am the light that includes all lights.
I am one with the Source, and the Source lives as me."

WHY THIS IS CROWN WORK (NOT ESCAPE)

Sahasrara is realized through life, not apart from it.
After the lotus opens, its nectar—amṛta—descends to nourish every chakra:

- Root feels safety in Being.
- Sacral feels joy without grasping.
- Solar Plexus acts with humble clarity.
- Heart loves with no opposite.
- Throat speaks with grace and truth.

- Third Eye rests in quiet knowing.

This is the completion of the yogic arc: not leaving the world, but lighting it from within.

The Descent of Light: How Sahasrara Nourishes the Lower Chakras

Enlightenment is not an escape upward; it is light returning downward.
When Sahasrara opens, the nectar of awareness—amṛta—flows through the crown and descends, blessing each chakra. Unity becomes embodiment. Stillness becomes service. Heaven becomes human.

Think of it as the two currents completing their circle:

- Ascending Shakti carries experience home to Source.
- Descending Shiva pours grace into form.
  Their union at the crown sends a gentle rain of light through the whole system.

CROWN → THIRD EYE (VIOLET TO INDIGO): LIGHT BECOMES CLEAR KNOWING

When the Crown is awake, insight at Ajna becomes quiet certainty—not hunches, not analysis, but lucid intuition free of fear.

- Nourishment: Unity clarifies perception; symbols and synchronicities align without strain.
- Healed distortions: Overthinking, projection, spiritual doubt.

- Practice: After meditation, rest in the *silence after OM*, then bring awareness to the brow and ask, "What is already known?" Receive—don't reach.

Affirmation: *"Because I am One, I see clearly."*

CROWN → THROAT (VIOLET TO BLUE): LIGHT BECOMES TRUE VOICE

Grace descends and the voice loses performance. Speech is clean, kind, and precise.

- Nourishment: Words carry resonance, not persuasion; listening deepens.
- Healed distortions: Over-talking, people-pleasing, withholding truth.
- Practice: On exhale, imagine white-violet light flowing from crown to throat. Speak only after one breath of silence.

Affirmation: *"Silence guides my words."*

CROWN → HEART (VIOLET TO GREEN): LIGHT BECOMES UNCONDITIONAL LOVE

Unity softens the chest; compassion no longer costs energy because it flows from Source, not self.

- Nourishment: Forgiveness feels natural; boundaries become clear and loving.
- Healed distortions: Attachment, rescuing, guardedness.
- Practice: Inhale through crown, exhale into heart; visualize a lotus opening and blessing someone (or yourself) without agenda.

Affirmation: *"One light beats every heart."*

CROWN → SOLAR PLEXUS (VIOLET TO GOLD): LIGHT BECOMES HUMBLE POWER

Purpose shifts from proving to serving. Will aligns with wisdom, action with ease.

- Nourishment: Decisions become effortless; courage is calm.
- Healed distortions: Control, burnout, indecision.
- Practice: After attuning at the crown, rest one hand on navel; ask, "What would Love like me to do?" Take the smallest clear step.

Affirmation: *"Power is light in motion."*

CROWN → SACRAL (VIOLET TO ORANGE): LIGHT BECOMES JOYFUL FLOW

Creativity is devotion. Desire is purified into delight without grasping.

- Nourishment: Play, sensual presence, art as prayer.
- Healed distortions: Craving, numbness, creative block.
- Practice: Breathe crown-to-pelvis; sway or draw slowly with eyes closed, letting movement be guided by inner pulse rather than goal.

Affirmation: *"The divine dances through me."*

CROWN → ROOT (VIOLET TO RED): LIGHT BECOMES LIVING GROUND

Unity anchors as felt safety. The body trusts the earth; presence is home.

- Nourishment: Stability, enoughness, simple gratitude.
- Healed distortions: Anxiety, scarcity, dissociation.

- Practice: Imagine white-violet rain descending to the soles of the feet. Walk slowly, repeating inwardly: *"This step is God."*

Affirmation: *"I am safely held by the One."*

The Circuit Completed: Upward Realization, Downward Blessing

When Sahasrara blossoms, the system organizes around coherence:

- The Root rests,
- the Sacral plays,
- the Solar Plexus serves,
- the Heart includes,
- the Throat rings true,
- the Third Eye knows,
- and the Crown abides.

This is not a ladder but a fountain. The more you let light descend, the more naturally it rises.

A Simple Daily Descent (5 minutes)

1. One Minute – Crown: Sit tall; feel space above the head. Whisper once, *"OM,"* then rest in the after-silence.
2. One Breath Each – Down the Centers:
   o Brow: *clarity*
   o Throat: *truth*
   o Heart: *love*
   o Solar Plexus: *service*
   o Sacral: *joy*
   o Root: *trust*
     With each exhale, imagine white-violet light landing in that center.

3. One Minute – Embody: Stand, feel feet; open your eyes into the world as temple.

When Descent is Blocked

- Feeling spacey? Send light to Root; eat, walk, touch earth.
- Inspired but anxious? Bring the Crown's silence to Solar Plexus; simplify the next step.
- Clear insights, hard conversations? Crown-to-Throat; breathe once before speaking.
- Compassion fatigue? Let light refill Heart before giving again.

Prayer of the Descent

Light that I am,
flow as clarity in my mind,
truth in my voice,
love in my heart,
service in my will,
joy in my body,
and trust in my steps.
Let heaven walk as earth through me.

THE TRANSCENDENCE OF FORM: THE CROWN'S LIVING SYMBOL

Unlike the lower chakras, Sahasrara has no animal guardian.
In yogic and Tantric tradition, each animal—elephant, antelope, ram, peacock—embodies the instinctual energy that fuels spiritual evolution.
But at the Crown, instinct has fulfilled its purpose. The journey of refinement is complete.
Sahasrara stands beyond form, beyond instinct, beyond duality.
It represents the state where energy no longer needs a vehicle—

where consciousness has realized itself as the source of all motion.

The Crown's guardian, therefore, is not a creature, but a creation—
the White or Thousand-Petaled Lotus, blooming eternally at the top of the subtle spine.
It is the emblem of pure awareness, each petal a ray of realization, unfolding without end.
The lotus grows from the mud of human experience, rises through the waters of emotion, and opens only in the light of divine understanding.
It needs no protector because it is protection itself—light that cannot be dimmed, truth that cannot be touched.

In the stillness of Sahasrara, the seeker and the sought dissolve.
Only the Lotus remains—radiant, timeless, and awake—
a symbol not of ascent, but of arrival:
the flowering of Spirit within matter,
the quiet knowing that all forms are simply petals of one infinite bloom.

THE ABSENCE OF ANIMAL SYMBOLISM

Sahasrara transcends the instinctual nature that the lower chakras refine and balance.
Therefore, it has no animal guardian, for instinct has completed its evolution.
At the Crown, energy no longer moves through desire or fear — it rests in realization.
The absence of a guardian here symbolizes liberation from form — the freedom of consciousness unbound.

THE DEITIES OF THE CROWN CHAKRA

(Sahasrara – The Infinite Lotus of Consciousness)

At the summit of the subtle body, where form dissolves into formlessness, Sahasrara stands beyond duality, beyond archetype, beyond even deity as we understand it.
In the Tantric cosmology, each of the lower chakras is animated by a divine intelligence — a guardian of energy, an archetypal force of creation.
But at the crown, divinity is no longer personified — it is experienced. Sahasrara is not presided over by a god or goddess, but by Pure Consciousness itself, radiant and infinite.

Yet, to help the human mind glimpse the inexpressible, the sages gave the ineffable form — luminous, symbolic, transcendent.

SHIVA – PURE CONSCIOUSNESS (PARAMA SHIVA)

At the crown resides Parama Shiva, the Absolute — the silent witness beyond sound, beyond thought, beyond time.
Here, awareness no longer identifies with body, mind, or self; it rests as pure being.
In this aspect, Shiva is not the destroyer, but the stillness from which all creation emanates and to which it returns.
He is the unmanifest field — consciousness untouched by form, the eternal void that births and absorbs all worlds.
Meditating upon Shiva at Sahasrara is not devotion to a deity, but surrender into the vastness of awareness.

"He who sees all beings in the Self, and the Self in all beings, never turns away from it." — *Isha Upanishad*

SHAKTI – THE DESCENDING GRACE (SHIVĀ ŚAKTI)

At the crown, Shiva is never alone. The stillness of consciousness meets the flow of energy — Shakti, the creative pulse of divine will.

When energy (Kundalinī Shakti) rises from the root to merge with Shiva at Sahasrara, the union of the two becomes bliss — *ānanda*.

In that merging, opposites dissolve: masculine and feminine, spirit and matter, light and shadow.

The yogi experiences not worship, but oneness — the eternal dance of stillness and motion as one heartbeat.

Here, Shakti is not a goddess apart, but the radiant light through which Shiva knows Himself.

The ancient texts call this state *Sat-Chit-Ānanda — Existence, Consciousness, Bliss.*

THE THOUSAND-PETALED LOTUS – EMBLEM OF INFINITY

Since the mind cannot hold infinity, the sages envisioned Sahasrara as a thousand-petaled lotus, opening endlessly toward the heavens.

Each petal symbolizes one vibration of divine consciousness — the infinite ways awareness expresses itself through creation.

It is white, violet, or opalescent, shimmering with all colors yet belonging to none.

The lotus is both the crown and the root of the subtle body — its roots in earth, its bloom in heaven, uniting matter and spirit.

When meditated upon, the lotus reveals itself not as a flower above the head, but as a state of being — awareness fully awake to itself.

In this awakening, every chakra beneath becomes illuminated by the same light; every breath becomes prayer; every moment becomes divine.

"The thousand-petaled lotus shines like lightning —
its radiance illumines the world within." — Shat-Chakra-
Nirupana

THE DEITY BEYOND DEITIES

If Ajna teaches us to see through the eyes of the soul, Sahasrara
teaches us to be the soul itself — luminous, infinite, and aware.
Its deity is no one and everyone — the nameless essence that
every tradition has tried to name:

- *The Brahman* of Vedanta — infinite existence-
  consciousness-bliss.
- *The Ain Soph* of Kabbalah — the limitless light.
- *The Godhead* of Christian mysticism — that which is
  beyond all image.
- *The Dharmakāya* of Buddhism — the body of absolute
  truth.

All are metaphors pointing to the same ineffable Source.
Sahasrara is that realization — the flowering of awareness
where all paths, all names, and all forms dissolve into silence.

"In the crown of light, the yogi becomes the sun itself —
shining, silent, one without a second."

The Biology Of Transcendence: The Crown Chakra And The Brain Of Light

While the Third Eye translates awareness into vision, the Crown Chakra represents consciousness itself — the field in which perception, energy, and intelligence unite.
Modern neuroscience offers a fascinating parallel: when Sahasrara awakens, the brain reflects it through coherence, integration, and light.

THE PREFRONTAL–PARIETAL NETWORK: THE NEUROLOGY OF UNITY

Advanced brain imaging of mystics and long-term meditators shows a distinctive pattern when they enter states of deep transcendence:

- Deactivation of the parietal lobes, which normally construct spatial boundaries and the sense of "self versus other."
- Heightened synchronization in the prefrontal cortex, which governs awareness, compassion, and decision-making.
  This combination produces the subjective experience of oneness — the hallmark of the Crown Chakra — where the boundaries of identity dissolve into universal consciousness.

In neurotheology, this is called unitary awareness, a measurable correlate of what yogic texts call *samādhi* — absorption in pure being.

THE THALAMUS: THE GATEWAY OF CONSCIOUSNESS

The thalamus, often described as the brain's relay hub, filters sensory input and directs information to the cortex.

During meditation or contemplative absorption, thalamic filtering relaxes, allowing subtler waves of perception to enter awareness.

This mirrors the yogic description of Sahasrara as the open gate — the thousand-petaled lotus through which consciousness communicates with the infinite.

When this gateway harmonizes with the pineal and pituitary glands, the entire nervous system resonates in rhythmic unity — a physiological expression of enlightenment.

NEURAL COHERENCE AND THE FIELD OF LIGHT

Research in biophysics and quantum biology reveals that the brain emits measurable biophotons — ultra-weak light pulses involved in cellular communication.

When the brain enters high coherence through meditation, these emissions increase in order and amplitude, forming patterns of rhythmic light.

Yogic masters long described this as the "inner radiance" or "bodiless light" perceived during deep samādhi — the glow of consciousness itself.

Science now recognizes this luminosity as a potential signature of neural synchronization — light as both messenger and metaphor for awareness.

THE VAGUS NERVE AND DESCENDING GRACE

The vagus nerve, running from brainstem to heart and organs, acts as the bridge between the Crown and the body.

When Sahasrara energy descends after awakening, it activates the parasympathetic response — slowing heart rate, deepening breath, and restoring harmony throughout the system.

This is the biological "descent of light": spirit entering form, bliss entering biology.

The yogi feels it as waves of peace and wholeness; neuroscience measures it as heart–brain coherence and vagal tone.

Both describe the same truth — that illumination, when embodied, becomes healing.

NEUROCHEMISTRY OF ECSTASY

During states of transcendence, studies show fluctuations in serotonin, endorphins, dopamine, and oxytocin — a biochemical symphony reflecting joy, trust, and connection.

Some researchers suggest that trace secretions from the pineal gland, possibly including dimethyltryptamine (DMT), may contribute to mystical vision.

Whether literal or symbolic, these neurochemical harmonies correspond to the yogic experience of *amṛta*, the nectar that descends from the Crown during enlightenment.

This "nectar" nourishes every chakra, stabilizing illumination within the body — a living physiology of bliss.

THE BRAIN IN MEDITATION: THE STILLNESS THAT SHINES

EEG and fMRI studies consistently show that deep meditation generates gamma-wave coherence — rapid, high-frequency patterns linked to expanded awareness and compassion.

In this state, the brain functions not as a separate organ but as a harmonic instrument of consciousness, vibrating in unity across all regions.

Sahasrara corresponds to this peak coherence — the crown of integration where thought ceases and knowing becomes direct.

The ancients called it *turiya*, the fourth state — beyond waking, dreaming, and deep sleep — pure awareness itself.

THE PHYSIOLOGY OF ENLIGHTENMENT

From a scientific perspective:

- The pineal gland senses light.
- The pituitary coordinates the body.
- The thalamus and cortex translate experience into meaning.
- But Sahasrara unites them all in a single symphony of coherence — awareness harmonizing its own creation.

From a spiritual perspective:

- The Crown Chakra is where consciousness knows itself as divine.
- It is not limited by biology, yet biology becomes its mirror.
- Light is both its symbol and its science — photons as particles of perception, awareness as the field that binds them.

When science meets spirit, both affirm the same mystery:
that illumination is not something that happens in the brain, but
something the brain learns to *reflect*.

THE BIOLOGICAL MIRROR OF THE THOUSAND-PETALED LOTUS

Just as the lotus opens endlessly toward light, the human brain
— with its billions of synapses — unfolds in ever finer
networks of connection.
Each petal mirrors a neural circuit; each spark of awareness, a
photon of divine intelligence.
The more coherent the network, the more radiant the
consciousness it carries.
Sahasrara, then, is the brain's full bloom — the living lotus of
light through which the universe perceives itself.

THE FINAL SYNTHESIS

From mysticism to neuroscience, all languages converge here:

- The yogi speaks of the thousand-petaled lotus.
- The mystic speaks of divine union.
- The physicist speaks of quantum coherence.
  All describe the same ascent — and descent — of awareness.

Sahasrara reveals that enlightenment is not escape from matter, but matter remembering its light.
In the biology of transcendence, the brain is not the source of consciousness — it is the instrument through which consciousness sings.

ARCHETYPES OF THE CROWN CHAKRA (SAHASRARA)

Every chakra expresses universal archetypes—living patterns of consciousness that reveal both our light and our shadow.
For Sahasrara, the Crown Chakra, archetypes point beyond identity to pure awareness and its gentle return into life as service.
Where Ajna sees and interprets, the Crown is—resting as the field in which seeing arises and to which it returns.

Sahasrara's current unfolds through two primary archetypes:
The Witness and The Vessel.

THE WITNESS

The Witness embodies the essence of the Crown: spacious, silent presence—awareness that includes everything and clings to nothing.
It is the knowing that remains when thought grows quiet; the sky in which all weather passes.

In Balance:

- Abides as peaceful, non-judging presence.
- Experiences unity without losing compassion for difference.
- Lets life move without grasping or rejecting; humility arises naturally.
- Loves all beings equally, not abstractly but intimately.

In Shadow:

- The Escapist: uses "oneness" to bypass feelings, responsibilities, or the body.
- The Nihilist: mistakes emptiness for meaninglessness; withdraws from life.
- The Aloof Mystic: confuses detachment with superiority; avoids intimacy.

Lesson of the Witness:
Transcend and include. Let vastness hold your humanity. True detachment is warm, not cold.

THE VESSEL

If the Witness realizes oneness, the Vessel embodies it—letting light descend as kindness, wisdom, and service.
The Vessel is the open channel through which grace becomes action.

In Balance:

- Serves without self-erasure; boundaries are clear and loving.
- Words, art, and choices feel guided, simple, and timely.
- Power is gentle; authority is shared; impact is blessing, not performance.

In Shadow:

- The Martyr: over-gives, burns out, confuses depletion with devotion.
- The Savior: assumes others' paths, rescues instead of empowers.
- The Chosen One: inflates spiritual identity, seeks specialness over service.

Lesson of the Vessel:
Let love flow through you, not from you alone. Service is sustainable when sourced in Source.

THE DEEPER LESSON

Sahasrara teaches that awakening is a two-way movement:

- Upward: consciousness remembers itself as infinite (The Witness).
- Downward: that remembrance becomes blessing in the world (The Vessel).

When these archetypes harmonize, transcendence becomes tenderness.
You do not leave life; you light it.

TOGETHER: THE WITNESS AND THE VESSEL

- The Witness offers spacious awareness—freedom from grasping.
- The Vessel offers embodied grace—love in motion.
  One realizes unity; the other radiates it.
  Together they fulfill Sahasrara's purpose: being as blessing.

LIVING ARCHETYPALLY (CROWN)

Notice which current is active:

- If you feel vast but distant, invite The Vessel—act in one small, kind way.
- If you feel loving but drained, return to The Witness— rest in silence until giving is effortless again.

Living the Crown is the art of resting as awareness and moving as love.

CROWN CHAKRA ARCHETYPE REFLECTION EXERCISE

Find quiet. Sit tall. Bring attention to the space above your head.
Breathe softly until a sense of spacious, luminous stillness emerges—like open sky.

Exploring The Witness

1. When do I most easily rest as awareness rather than as my roles?
2. Where do I use "spiritual perspective" to avoid feeling or repair?
3. What helps me hold pain (mine/others') with warmth instead of withdrawal?
4. How can I let silence companion me in everyday tasks?

Exploring The Vessel

1. Where is life inviting me to serve simply and sustainably?
2. What boundaries would make my giving clearer and kinder?
3. Do I help to be helpful—or to be needed?

4. What practice reliably reconnects my action to Source (prayer, mantra, nature, stillness)?

Integration

- Which archetype needs nurturing today—Witness or Vessel?
- One gentle step I'll take to balance transcendence with embodiment is: _____.

REFLECTION MANTRA (SAHASRARA)

"I rest as the Witness—vast, silent, one.
I move as the Vessel—gentle, grounded, kind.
Light is my nature; love is my way."

Chapter 3 – The Energetic Blueprint of the Crown Chakra

The Crown Chakra and the Aura

The Crown Chakra (Sahasrara) is not merely the seat of spiritual connection — it is the luminous field of pure consciousness, the gateway through which individual awareness merges with the infinite.
If the Third Eye refines perception into insight, then the Crown transcends perception altogether — dissolving seer, seeing, and seen into one radiant stillness.
Here, light no longer reflects — it *emanates.*
Consciousness does not reach for understanding; it *becomes* understanding itself.

When Sahasrara is open and balanced, the aura surrounding the crown of the head glows with hues of violet, gold, white, and soft opalescent light — an ever-shifting iridescence that feels both vast and intimate.
This light extends upward like a fountain of subtle flame or a halo, merging seamlessly with the higher auric layers and the universal field of divine intelligence.
It is as though the individual's energy ceases to end — dissolving into infinity while remaining centered in peace.

Others sense this as serenity, compassion, and a profound stillness that needs no words.
The presence of a balanced Crown feels like being near an open

sky — limitless, quiet, and deeply safe.
It emanates coherence — an alignment of all lower chakras into unity.
Every vibration within the energy body harmonizes around this central silence, creating an aura that hums with peace.

When Sahasrara is radiant, one moves through life not as a seeker, but as the presence of the divine realized.
Awareness flows effortlessly through every layer of being —

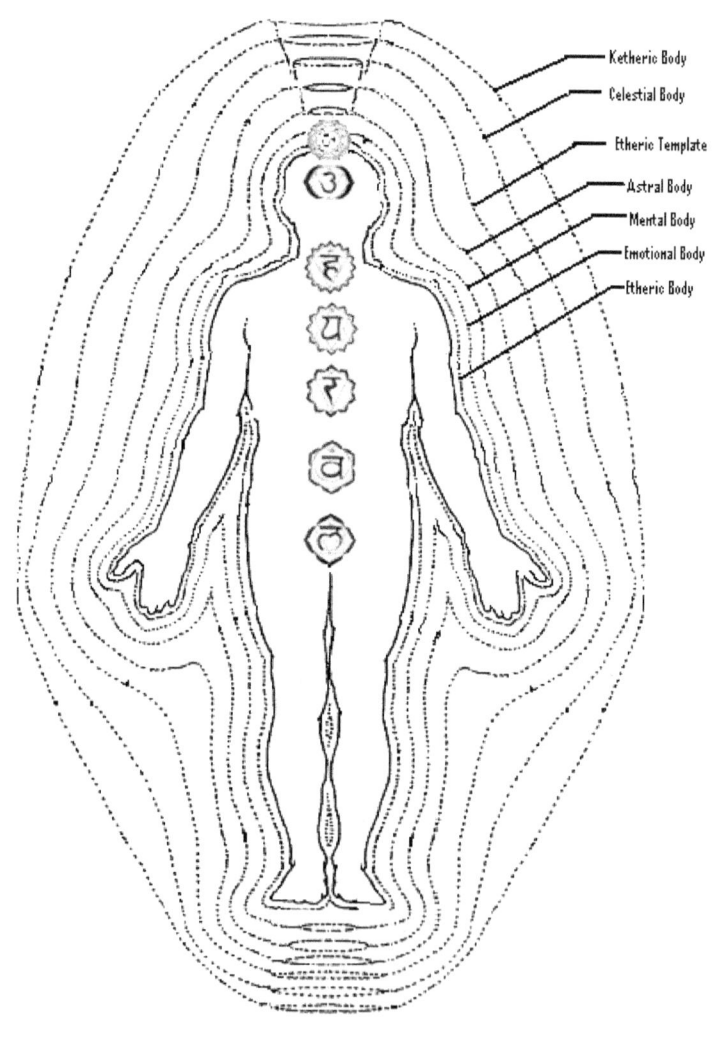

Ketheric Body
Celestial Body
Etheric Template
Astral Body
Mental Body
Emotional Body
Etheric Body

thought, emotion, and action illuminated by the same quiet brilliance.
This is the field of enlightenment — consciousness awake to itself.

THE CROWN AS THE RADIANT FIELD OF UNITY

The Crown Chakra acts as the transcendent halo of the energy field — the point where the auric body opens into the universal matrix of light.
Unlike the other chakras, which channel specific frequencies of expression, the Crown radiates pure vibration — undifferentiated awareness beyond polarity.
It is the zero point of consciousness — silence pregnant with creation.

When balanced, the entire aura becomes luminous and coherent, pulsing gently with the rhythm of divine order.
Meditation, prayer, and moments of awe naturally attune the Crown to this vibration.
The energy feels like an infinite expansion — light without boundary, consciousness without effort.

Practices such as resting awareness above the head, visualizing a thousand-petaled lotus, or silently chanting OM or SO HAM harmonize the subtle currents with the Source field.
These practices affirm the living truth:

"I am light. I am consciousness. I am one with all that is."

In this resonance, the aura becomes crystalline — transparent and radiant, shimmering like dew in morning sunlight.
The field's boundaries soften; the personal merges with the universal, and individuality reveals itself as a facet of the whole.

THE AURA OF LIGHT: SAHASRARA'S LUMINOSITY

When Sahasrara is open, a column of light often extends from the crown into the higher dimensions of the subtle field — a golden-white beam connecting heaven and earth through the human form.
This light is not static but gently pulsates in rhythm with the heart and breath, merging the personal life force with the greater cosmic pulse.

Energetically, this radiance appears as fine, mist-like filaments of white or violet light interwoven with gold — delicate yet powerful, serene yet dynamic.
It is the vibration of enlightenment: awareness resting as itself.
In this state, the aura becomes a living mandala of coherence.
Its texture is still, smooth, and luminous — a reflection of divine equilibrium within human form.

When this chakra is blocked or dormant, the aura may appear compressed or dim above the head.
One may feel spiritually disconnected, lost in intellect, or unable to experience meaning or faith.
This is the state of separation consciousness — awareness identified with form rather than essence.
When overactive, the energy may rise too quickly, leaving the body ungrounded or overwhelmed by transcendence — a state of spiritual dissociation.
Balance is found in integration: letting light descend gently through all chakras, rooting heaven into earth.

THE QUALITY OF LIGHT

Sahasrara's element is not earth, water, fire, air, or even ether — it is pure light itself.
This is the frequency of *jyoti*, the divine radiance from which all forms emerge and to which all return.
Its light appears as white shot through with violet, gold, and

silver, or as a translucent shimmer that seems both visible and invisible.

This light does not illuminate objects — it illuminates *being*.
It reveals not the world, but the consciousness in which the world appears.
It is awareness perceiving itself, infinite and indivisible.

Those attuned to this vibration often radiate tranquility.
Their presence feels luminous and soft, yet unmistakably powerful — like sunlight diffused through mist.
The energy field around them communicates peace that transcends words — the silent assurance that *all is one.*

THE FIELD OF DIVINE CONNECTION

Through Sahasrara, energy flows upward and outward into the infinite — connecting the human biofield to the universal energy grid.
This is the apex of the Kundalini current, where the ascending life force unites with divine consciousness.
The thousand-petaled lotus opens, and awareness no longer alternates between the finite and the infinite — it rests as both.

When this flow is open, divine inspiration, guidance, and synchronicity arise effortlessly.
The mind becomes luminous and clear, intuitive knowing arises without seeking, and the heart remains anchored in peace.
The aura resonates as an electromagnetic symphony of coherence, mirroring the cosmic order itself.
It is here that the human field vibrates at the frequency of unconditional unity.

THE DESCENT OF LIGHT

Though energy ascends through the chakras, Sahasrara also opens the downward current — the descent of light.
Once union is realized, awareness begins its return journey: spirit infusing matter, consciousness illuminating creation.
This descent completes the cycle of evolution — heaven entering earth through the awakened human vessel.
The individual becomes a conduit of divine grace — not as an idea, but as a living energy that blesses and balances all it touches.

In this sacred reciprocity, the aura becomes a radiant bridge — channeling divine light through form into the world.
Healing, insight, creativity, and compassion flow naturally as expressions of unity.

THE ESSENCE OF THE CROWN FIELD

The energetic blueprint of the Crown Chakra is the template of wholeness — the remembrance that separation is illusion.
Where the lower chakras manage individuality, Sahasrara reveals universality.
It is the field through which consciousness recognizes itself in all beings, all forms, all times.

When fully awakened, you no longer "have" an aura — you are the aura: an infinite field of luminous awareness temporarily expressing through form.
Your very presence becomes transmission — the silent radiance of unity embodied.

"Light does not travel; it simply shines.
The Crown does not reach upward; it opens outward into infinity."

This is the essence of Sahasrara — the final flowering of the subtle body, where illumination becomes embodiment and being becomes bliss.

MODERN CHALLENGES TO SAHASRARA (THE CROWN CHAKRA)

In our hyper-connected world, the Crown is often veiled not by ignorance, but by overload.
We scroll endlessly, sleep fitfully, and worship productivity while neglecting stillness.
Algorithms curate our attention; hurry hardens our nervous systems.
The result is a subtle severance: information without meaning, activity without essence, connection without communion.

Common disruptors of the Crown current:

- Chronic stimulation & sleep debt: irregular light exposure, late-night screens, and fractured rest dull the nervous system's receptivity to silence.
- Cynicism & hyper-materialism: reducing reality to what can be measured alone collapses wonder and numbs reverence.
- Spiritual bypassing: using "oneness" to avoid feeling, repairing, or relating—transcendence without tenderness.
- Isolation & disembodiment: digital closeness without embodied presence; living "in the head," unrooted in heart and earth.
- Meaning fragmentation: ceaseless novelty erodes contemplation; there is no time for insight to ripen into wisdom.

Healing the Crown is not more content—it is more contact: with silence, with breath, with earth, with one another, with the Presence that underlies all things.

RESTORING THE CROWN CURRENT

Rhythms of Light & Rest

- Honor circadian light: sunrise on your skin, screens dim after dusk.
- Keep a consistent sleep/wake window; protect the hour before bed as blue-light sabbath.
- Let darkness be sacrament—silence, candles, a single star.

Sacred Pause

- Daily minutes of wordless sitting above the crown; feel the space opening like a thousand-petaled lotus.
- End meditation with descent of light—crown to brow, throat, heart, navel, sacral, root—so unity becomes embodiment.

Embodied Reverence

- Place bare feet on ground; breathe slowly until the heart and breath agree.
- Choose one ordinary act (making tea, washing hands) as a living prayer.

Community & Service

- Replace abstraction with small mercies: a check-in, a meal shared, a kindness offered.
- Service grounds transcendence; grace becomes practical.

Meaning Practices

- Gratitude, sacred reading, chant, contemplative prayer or mantra (e.g., *So'ham, OM*).

- Keep a "traces of grace" journal—one sentence a day where the Infinite showed itself in the ordinary.

THE LIGHT OF UNITY

When Sahasrara balances, the aura crowns in opalescent white-violet—soft, measureless, serene.
You no longer strive to belong to the world; you belong to Being itself.
Understanding is no longer chased—it arrives.
Action is no longer forced—it flows.

Here, the Crown becomes a quiet sun:

- Thought slows and clarifies.
- Compassion widens without effort.
- Presence gathers—rooms grow calm, conversations soften, choices simplify.

To honor Sahasrara is to remember: silence is intelligent, stillness is generous, unity is practical. What descends from the Crown must feed the roots of life—words kinder, work cleaner, love steadier.

A UNIVERSAL UNDERSTANDING OF TRANSCENDENCE

Though the chakra map is yogic, the experience of unitary presence is human and perennial.

Indigenous Wisdom
Great Spirit, Creator, Sky Father / Earth Mother—languages of kinship with the one life in many forms. Ceremony returns time to sacred rhythm; community restores the circle.

Vedanta & Tantra
Brahman—existence-consciousness-bliss without a second.

Shiva–Shakti—stillness and power as one pulse. Sahasrara is the lotus where they marry in awareness.

Buddhist Mysticism
Dharmakāya—the formless body of truth. Emptiness is not void but vastness; compassion arises naturally when self/other dissolves.

Christian Contemplative Stream
"The Cloud of Unknowing," apophatic prayer: God beyond image, met in loving silence. The crown opens where concepts end and communion begins.

Kabbalah
Ein Sof—the Limitless Light. From the unbounded Source, emanations flow; ascent returns as descent of blessing through the tree of life.

Sufi Path
Nūr 'alā Nūr—"Light upon Light." The polished heart reflects the One; remembrance (*dhikr*) reveals the crown as ever-present radiance.

Across paths, the lesson converges: The One is not somewhere else. The One is what you are.

CROSS-CULTURAL EMBODIMENT OF CROWN LIGHT

- Sabbath & Simplicity: sacred pauses that re-enthrone being over doing.
- Pilgrimage & Nature: walking until the mind gets quiet enough to hear.
- Chant & Breath: vibration softens thought; breath escorts you to the threshold.
- Rituals of Gratitude: bowing before meals, at doorways, to morning light.

- Blessing as Practice: silently "May you be held" to those you pass—unity made useful.

THE SACRED LIGHT OF SAHASRARA

Light at the Crown is not the light that shines on things, but the light that shines as things.
It is the field in which stars, feelings, and ideas appear and disappear without remainder.
To live from Sahasrara is to let life move through you as grace—unclenched, unafraid, unanxious for outcome.

Universal lesson of the Crown:

- Unity awakens.
- Unity reveals.
- Unity reconciles.

When the crown is clear, you don't abandon the world; you brighten it.
Silence becomes guidance. Presence becomes blessing.
And the thousand-petaled lotus keeps opening—
petal by petal— until there is no distance left between light and life.

How Practitioners Work With The Crown Chakra

For healers and energy practitioners, the Crown Chakra —
Sahasrara — represents the summit of consciousness: the
gateway to divine intelligence and the remembrance of unity
with all life.
Located at the top of the head, it governs spiritual connection,
higher understanding, and the descent of divine light into the
human experience.
Where the Third Eye translates intuition into perception, the
Crown dissolves perception into pure awareness.
It is not the eye that sees, but the light that makes seeing
possible.

When Sahasrara is balanced, the individual feels guided,
peaceful, and open to the flow of divine wisdom.
Thought becomes clear yet spacious, and life feels
interconnected — infused with meaning and grace.
When blocked or closed, one may feel disconnected from
purpose, spiritually adrift, or overly rational and skeptical.
In overactivity, there may be disassociation, escapism, or
difficulty grounding insights into everyday life.

ASSESSMENT

Practitioners begin by sensing the client's relationship with
faith, meaning, and trust in the unseen.
They may explore questions such as:

- Do you feel connected to something greater than
  yourself?
- Are you open to spiritual guidance, or do you rely solely
  on logic and control?
- Do you experience feelings of isolation, confusion about
  purpose, or existential fatigue?

- Are you grounded in daily life, or do you feel "spaced out" or unanchored?
- How do you experience stillness, silence, or prayer? Do they comfort or unsettle you?

Energetically, healers perceive the Crown as a field of white, gold, or violet light radiating upward and outward from the top of the head.
This radiance merges with the universal field of consciousness, reflecting how open the individual is to divine flow.

- A balanced Crown feels luminous, serene, and boundless — energy flowing both upward and downward with ease.
- An underactive Crown may feel dull, flat, or constricted — as if the top of the head is sealed or energetically heavy.
- An overactive Crown may feel overstimulated or flickering — light that rises too quickly, leaving the body depleted or ungrounded.

Practitioners also observe how Sahasrara integrates with Ajna (Third Eye) and Anahata (Heart) — the three higher centers of spiritual synthesis.
When aligned, wisdom flows effortlessly: insight becomes compassion, and compassion becomes embodiment.
When misaligned, disconnection occurs — spiritual insight without grounding, or intellect without illumination.

ENERGY HEALING TECHNIQUES
Reiki & Hands-On Healing

The practitioner channels energy into and above the Crown, often hovering hands two to four inches above the head.
White or violet light is visualized descending gently into the body, harmonizing the entire chakra column.
This re-establishes flow between the higher consciousness and

physical form — heaven meeting earth through the human vessel.

Light Infusion Meditation

The practitioner guides the client to visualize a thousand-petaled lotus above the head, each petal opening as light streams downward.
This descent of illumination clears energetic residue from the aura and infuses every cell with divine frequency.
It is not about "reaching up," but about allowing light to enter and integrate.

Sound & Frequency Healing

The bija mantra OM or AUM aligns Sahasrara with the vibration of universal consciousness.
Toning OM or using crystal bowls in the key of B creates a subtle resonance that unifies all chakras and stills the mind.
Practitioners may also work in silence, using the absence of sound as a medium of transmission.

Crystal Healing

Clear quartz, selenite, diamond, and amethyst are among the primary stones used for Crown work.
Placed above the head or along the crown line, these stones amplify clarity, purification, and divine alignment.
Selenite, in particular, is used to clear energetic residue and invite the descent of higher light into the field.

Aromatherapy

Sacred oils such as lotus, frankincense, myrrh, and rose support transcendence, devotion, and peace.
Diffused or applied lightly at the crown, they act as bridges

between body and spirit — their fragrance lifting consciousness into serenity.

BODYWORK PRACTICES

Though the Crown is ethereal, its health depends on embodiment. Practitioners anchor high-frequency work through gentle, grounding techniques.

- Scalp and Cranial Massage: Slow circular motion across the scalp releases tension and opens the crown point, allowing energy to flow through the skull and into the nervous system.
- Neck and Shoulder Release: Releasing muscular tension in the neck ensures the "gateway" remains open between the brainstem, spine, and crown.
- Energy Grounding through Feet and Legs: Always conclude crown work by directing energy downward — through the spine into the soles — to maintain balance and integration.
- Restorative Yoga: Supported poses such as Legs-Up-the-Wall (Viparita Karani) or Corpse Pose (Savasana) allow the nervous system to receive higher frequencies without overstimulation.

The aim is not to expand endlessly upward, but to circulate light through the whole body.

SPIRITUAL & ANCESTRAL HEALING

Sahasrara connects not only to divine consciousness but also to ancestral and collective evolution.
Many carry inherited energetic patterns of spiritual fear, religious trauma, or separation from Source.
Healing the Crown involves restoring the trust in the sacred — that divinity is not distant but immanent.

Common practices include:

- Golden Light Lineage Clearing: Visualizing a pillar of light descending through the family line, washing away fear, guilt, or distortion tied to spiritual misunderstanding.
- Soul Reconnection Meditation: Guiding clients to meet their Higher Self — the aspect of consciousness that remains eternally connected to the Divine.
- Prayer or Mantra Transmission: Repeating sacred phrases such as "I am one with the Light" or "All is within the One" to re-pattern belief from separation to unity.
- Celestial Grid Work: Practitioners may sense the client's energy connecting to a larger lattice of light — symbolic of the soul's belonging to the greater whole of creation.

These practices reawaken remembrance: that enlightenment is not a reward but a recognition of what has always been true.

INTEGRATION AND PRACTICE

Healing Sahasrara is less about ascension and more about embodiment of unity.
Practitioners emphasize the descent of divine energy through all chakras — allowing awareness to flow into action, compassion, and creativity.

Daily Practices to Support the Crown:

- Begin each morning in silence. Place your hands above your head and whisper:
  "I am the light of consciousness, grounded in grace."
- Practice gratitude as devotion — see every task, conversation, and challenge as an expression of the divine within form.

- Meditate with soft focus above the crown, then trace that light through the heart and into the earth.
- Keep a "moments of grace" journal — noting experiences of synchronicity, peace, or quiet knowing.
- Spend time under open sky. Let the vastness mirror your own.
- Balance spiritual study with embodied living — eat well, rest deeply, move mindfully.
  Illumination must feed life, not replace it.

When Sahasrara is open, awareness becomes effortless.
The practitioner's presence itself transmits peace — a living bridge between heaven and earth.
Healing at this level is not doing, but being; not directing, but allowing.

Through Sahasrara, we remember that enlightenment is not an escape from the human, but the sanctification of it — the divine recognizing itself through form.

"You are not a seeker of light.
You are the light through which God remembers being human."

Chapter 4 – Signs of Imbalance

Shadow Aspects of the Crown Chakra (Sahasrara)

Every chakra holds both light and shadow.
The Crown Chakra — Sahasrara — is the halo of pure awareness, the portal where individuality remembers its oneness with all that is.
When balanced, it confers a felt sense of grace, meaning, and belonging to the Whole. Silence becomes nourishment; guidance arrives as gentle knowing; life is permeated with reverence.

When misaligned, its current either dims into separation or over-expands into dissociation. We feel cut off from the sacred, or we float above the body without anchoring insight in daily life. These shadows are invitations to embody unity — to let the light descend and root, not only ascend and escape.

DISCONNECTION & EXISTENTIAL NUMBNESS (UNDERACTIVE SAHASRARA)

When the Crown is underactive, the world can feel flat, arbitrary, or godless.

- Signs: loss of meaning or faith, spiritual apathy, cynicism; a pervasive loneliness even when surrounded by others; resistance to silence or prayer.

- Energetic feel: the crown "cap" feels heavy, sealed, or dull; the field above the head appears dim or collapsed.
- Body cues: fatigue, brain fog, low mood, tension at the crown/occiput, restless sleep.

Healing direction: Begin with *gentle devotion*. Sit in quiet morning light, practice gratitude, walk under open sky. Whisper simple prayers or mantras ("I am held"). Invite wonder back through beauty: music, poetry, nature. Let small rituals rethread meaning.

SPIRITUAL ESCAPISM & DISSOCIATION (OVERACTIVE SAHASRARA)

When the Crown overfires, light outruns embodiment. One "lives upstairs," bypassing human feeling and responsibility.

- Signs: disconnection from the body, aversion to needs and limits, using spirituality to avoid grief/anger; chasing peak states, neglecting relationships or livelihood.
- Energetic feel: a bright, flickering field above the head, but thin through the torso and legs; insight without warmth.
- Body cues: dizziness, spaciness, insomnia, irregular appetite, cold extremities.

Healing direction: *Come down and in.* Eat warm, grounding foods; stand barefoot on earth; slow, weighted movement (yin yoga, mindful strength). After meditation, place hands on heart and belly: "Light, live here." Service and simple kindness anchor illumination in action.

DOGMA, RIGID BELIEF & MISPLACED AUTHORITY

Sahasrara imbalance can fixate on certainty — the mind clings to cosmologies to avoid the mystery.

- Signs: spiritual superiority, "one true path" thinking, dismissing others' experiences, and outsourcing authority to gurus or systems.
- Root wound: fear of the unknown and the vulnerability of true surrender.

Healing direction: Practice *humble not-knowing*. Sit in silence with questions unanswered. Read across traditions. Ask: "Does this belief make me kinder, freer, more present?" Let truth be known by its fruit.

SEVERED HEAD / CLOSED HEART: SPLIT OF CROWN FROM HEART

Light without love can be cold; love without light can be lost.

- Signs: refined metaphysics but little empathy; insight that doesn't translate to relationship; compassion fatigue.
- Healing direction: Breathe from crown to heart on the inhale, heart to crown on the exhale. Tonglen, devotional singing, and gratitude for a specific person daily. Unity must feel like tenderness.

PURPOSE VOID & LOSS OF CALLING

When the Crown dims, vocation feels accidental, or nothing feels "chosen."

- Signs: drifting, chronic second-guessing, envy of others' paths.

- Healing direction: Trade destiny panic for *daily devotion*. Offer one ordinary act each day as a sacred service. Purpose grows where love is consistently placed.

MENTAL OVERREACH: COSMIC IDEATION WITHOUT INTEGRATION

The mind tries to grasp the Infinite and tires itself.

- Signs: compulsive metaphysical speculation, serial course-hopping, prophetic inflation; little follow-through.
- Healing direction: Choose one practice for 40 days. Journal "light → life:" each insight must become one concrete act of kindness, repair, or creation.

PARADOX PANIC: FEAR OF MYSTERY

The crown opens into paradox — unity and diversity, emptiness and fullness. Unsteady nervous systems resist.

- Signs: anxiety in silence, agitation when practices deepen, spiritual experiences followed by backlash.
- Healing direction: Micro-doses of stillness. 3–5 minutes a day of receptive silence, then ground (tea, sun on skin). Build capacity for awe.

THE HIDDEN WOUND OF SAHASRARA

At the heart of Crown imbalance is a wound of belonging to the Whole. Somewhere, the soul learned that trusting the Larger Life was unsafe — that being guided meant losing control, or that love could vanish.

Healing is remembrance: not climbing to heaven, but letting heaven touch the human. The medicine is *receiving* — letting grace land in breath, body, and calendar. Unity realized is unity lived.

EMOTIONAL, MENTAL, SPIRITUAL & PHYSICAL SIGNS

Emotional: quiet grief or vague homesickness; irritability at "pointless" tasks; or, in overactivity, detachment and coolness.
Mental: meaning-crisis, nihilism, or on the flip side, hyper-abstract thinking and grand conclusions.
Spiritual: prayer feels dry; or experiences are frequent but unintegrated; rejection of practices that involve humility or service.
Physical: crown/occipital tension, sleep disruption, vestibular wobbliness; in depletion, low vitality; in excess, wired-and-tired.

IMBALANCE PATTERNS & REMEDIES

Underactive (Separation):

- Pattern: disbelief, numbness, isolation.
- Remedy: simple rituals, nature immersion, communal song/prayer, gratitude practice, gentle routine.

Overactive (Unanchored Light):

- Pattern: dissociation, bypass, fixation on peak states.
- Remedy: grounding foods, weighted movement, nervous-system downshifting, service, time limits on practice followed by embodiment.

Rigid/Dogmatic:

- Pattern: spiritual certainty that narrows compassion.
- Remedy: interfaith reading, listening circles, contemplative silence, "beginner's mind" vows.

Head–Heart Split:

- Pattern: clarity without kindness.
- Remedy: compassion practices, loving-kindness, crown-to-heart breath, relational repair.

THE CROWN'S CORE LESSON

Sahasrara teaches surrendered participation: not abandoning the human for the divine, but allowing the divine to be human through you.
Light fulfilled is light embodied — presence, kindness, right relationship, quiet joy.

When the Crown is healed, unity is ordinary.
Dishes are prayer, work is offering, silence is home.

MICRO-PRACTICES FOR REBALANCING

- Descent of Light (3 minutes):
  Inhale as if light rests a hand above your head; exhale, let it flow down through heart, belly, legs, and into the earth. End with one grounded action (glass of water, short walk).
- Sky & Soil:
  One hand on the crown, one on the lower belly. Breathe until both hands feel included. Say: *"I belong to sky and soil."*
- Devotion in Doing:
  Choose one mundane task as daily liturgy. Do it slowly, gratefully. Invite grace to inhabit the ordinary.
- Limits as Love:
  If overstimulated, cap formal practice time and always close with grounding (food, warmth, human contact).

THE DEEPER LESSON

Sahasrara's shadow is forgetting. Its healing is remembering —
not as an idea, but as a felt continuity with all life.
You do not have to reach the light.
You are the lamp, and your life is the oil.

When the Crown rests in balance, there is no drama around
awakening — only a quiet, continuous yes: to breath, to being,
to belonging.

Chapter 5 – Causes of Disturbance

Childhood Conditioning and the Loss of Sacred Belonging (Sahasrara)

If the Root teaches us that life is safe, the Sacral that life can be felt, the Solar Plexus that life can be directed, the Heart that life can be loved, and the Third Eye that life can be seen clearly, then the Crown Chakra — Sahasrara teaches us that life is holy. It is the remembrance that existence is meaningful, that we belong to something vast, tender, and intelligent.

Sahasrara begins to whisper early — in awe before a night sky, in the hush that follows a lullaby, in the first wonder at "where did I come from?" Its healthy development depends on trust, reverence, and welcome: caregivers who allow silence, honor mystery, and model a gentle relationship with the unseen. When supported, a child learns: *I am part of a living Whole. I am held. I can rest in something larger than me.*

When that environment is absent or distorted, the Crown's petals tighten. The child learns that the world is only mechanical or punitive, that silence is dangerous, that wonder is naïve. The result is an adult who either feels severed from meaning or floats above life in ungrounded transcendence — swinging between emptiness and escape.

MATERIALISM & SACRED AMNESIA

Message received: "Only what you can count is real."
Childhoods saturated in productivity, metrics, and performance
often train the psyche to distrust the invisible. Rituals vanish;
awe is replaced by achievement.

Adult pattern: chronic meaning-crisis, spiritual numbness, a
low-grade loneliness that success can't soothe.

Healing direction: reintroduce wonder in small, bodily ways —
dawn light, shared meals, simple blessings, a minute of silent
gratitude. Let meaning be *felt* before it is understood.

AUTHORITARIAN RELIGION & SPIRITUAL SHAME

Message received: "The Divine is far away, conditional, and
watching to punish."
When spiritual authority is externalized and weaponized,
children learn that direct experience is suspect and that
unworthiness is holy.

Adult pattern: fear of surrender, guilt around joy, outsourcing
guidance to gurus/systems, rejection of inner communion.

Healing direction: replace fear with friendship. Short, sincere
prayers ("Be with me."), quiet sitting, compassionate theology,
and community that values conscience as much as creed.

TRAUMA & FRAGMENTATION (DISSOCIATION UPWARD)

Message received: "It isn't safe to be here."
Shock, neglect, or chronic stress can propel awareness "up and
out." Light chases escape instead of incarnation.

Adult pattern: mystical sensitivity without stability, peak-state chasing, trouble sleeping, difficulty receiving comfort, body as an afterthought.

Healing direction: descent of light. Ground first (food, warmth, weighted rest), then contemplate. End every practice by drawing awareness down: crown → heart → belly → feet. Unity must land.

CONDITIONAL LOVE & THE WOUND OF UNWORTHINESS

Message received: "You earn love."
When acceptance depends on grades, piety, or perfection, the Crown equates worth with performance.

Adult pattern: spiritual perfectionism, "not holy enough" fatigue, inability to rest, treating practice like a ladder rather than a home.

Healing direction: devotion over achievement. Choose one tiny, daily offering (a candle, a thank-you, a breath at the window) and let it be enough.

INTELLECTUALIZATION & CYNICISM

Message received: "Mystery is for the foolish."
Brilliant homes that mock reverence create quick minds and closed heavens.

Adult pattern: elegant arguments, empty heart; relentless analysis of meaning with no felt participation in it.

Healing direction: let the head bow to the heart. Read poetry out loud. Sing. Study *and* sit. Ask, "Does this knowing make me kinder?"

FAMILY SECRETS & BROKEN TRUST IN LIFE

Message received: "Don't trust what you feel. Don't name what you see."
Gaslighting, secrecy, and betrayal fracture the capacity to relax into the Larger Holding.

Adult pattern: hypervigilance with the Divine, difficulty trusting grace, waiting for the other shoe to drop.

Healing direction: truth restores trust. Name what was hidden (gently, without blame). Practice being held — supportive touch, safe community, lying on the earth, guided relaxations that end with "You are carried."

OVERSTIMULATION, NOISE & THE EROSION OF RITUAL

Message received: "There is no time for silence."
Always-on inputs fray the Crown's filament.

Adult pattern: attention scattered, prayer dry, inability to savor, preference for novelty over depth.

Healing direction: ritualize pauses. One tech-free hour weekly. A screen-sabbath window. Candle at dusk. Let nervous-system quiet be the new altar.

CONTROL, CERTAINTY & FEAR OF NOT-KNOWING

Message received: "Safety is certainty."
The Crown opens into paradox; control clenches it shut.

Adult pattern: rigid cosmologies, spiritual policing, dread in the face of silence, clinging to systems that shrink compassion.

Healing direction: practice holy agnosticism. Sit with a question for 7 days without answering it. Measure truth by its fruit: more humility, more tenderness, more presence.

GRIEF UNMET & LOSS WITHOUT MEANING

Message received: "Move on."
Unmourned grief closes the skylight.

Adult pattern: bitterness toward life/God, avoidance of quiet, cynicism at other people's joy.

Healing direction: grief as sacrament — memory altars, names spoken, tears welcomed, community witnessing. Grief reopens the gate to communion.

INHERITED PATTERNS (ANCESTRAL / COLLECTIVE)

- Persecution & vows of silence: lineages punished for heterodoxy pass down fear of direct experience.
  Remedy: "I am safe to know the Holy within." Light a candle for those who could not.
- Authoritarian dogma: families equating obedience with holiness bequeath deference and doubt of inner truth.
  Remedy: reclaim sovereignty kindly: "I honor tradition and my own conscience."
- Exile/war/displacement: vigilance became salvation; now it mutes receptivity.
  Remedy: body safety first; crown work second. When the body trusts, heaven returns.
- Arrogance of certainty: knowledge wielded as power hardens the halo.
  Remedy: wonder training — star-gazing, beginner's mind, listening circles, interfaith hospitality.

CULTURAL DRIVERS

Productivity culture (worth = output), attention economies (no silence), and transactional spirituality (buy a peak state) all distort Sahasrara. The cure is embarrassingly simple: shared meals, shared songs, shared silence, shared service. Unity practiced, not purchased.

THE LASTING IMPACT

When the Crown is wounded, life feels unrelated: events without thread, self without Source. Or we ascend without arriving — light that never lands. Either way, the soul tires.

Healing Sahasrara is not about reaching higher. It is about receiving deeper — letting grace saturate breath, schedule, and skin; letting unity become ordinary.

HEALING MOVEMENTS (BRIEF PRESCRIPTIVES)

- Descent of Grace: After any practice, place one hand on crown, one on heart. Inhale "I receive," exhale "I belong."
- Ritualizing the Ordinary: Choose one daily act as liturgy (pouring tea, opening a window). Do it slowly, gratefully.
- Community & Service: Join a circle that prays/sings/sits; offer one quiet act of service weekly. Illumination becomes human when it feeds someone.
- Nature Communion: Morning sky or evening stars, three breaths of awe.
- Limit the Ladder: One path, 40 days. Depth over sampling. Close with food, warmth, human contact.

THE DEEPER LESSON

Sahasrara's core distortion is forgetting that you are already connected. Its medicine is remembrance lived. Not theory. Not peak. Presence.

You are not required to hold up the heavens.
You are invited to be held by them.

When the Crown rests in balance, meaning is not "found" — it is felt. Silence is friendly. Service is natural. And light no longer escapes upward; it descends into your words, your work, your touch — turning a single, ordinary day into a thousand-petaled prayer.

Environmental & Energetic Toxins At The Crown

Distraction, Deception, and the Loss of Living Communion (Sahasrara)

Sahasrara is the halo of belonging—the thousand-petaled openness through which Being knows itself as One. If Ajna refines sight, the Crown sanctifies what is seen: it dissolves separation and rests awareness in grace.
In a world of neon nights, monetized attention, and performative "spirituality," the crown field is pulled thin— connection traded for spectacle, reverence for rhetoric. The result is a quiet famine of meaning. We scroll, succeed, even "spiritually optimize," yet feel strangely unheld.

When the Crown dims, life seems unrelated: moments don't speak to each other; prayer feels like speaking into air. When it overfires without grounding, we float—bright ideas, brittle hearts.

THE REACTIVE NATURE OF SAHASRARA

The element of the Crown is pure consciousness—silent, lucid, unhurried. It thrives on stillness, sincerity, and simple awe. Toxins for this center aren't only chemical; they are existential:

- Noise & speed: perpetual urgency that makes silence feel unsafe.
- Cynicism & irony: reflexes that mock tenderness and mystery.
- Idolized intellect: cleverness without humility, analysis without adoration.
- Transactional spirituality: peak-state chasing, status masquerading as sanctity.

Under these, the crown either contracts (numb, faithless, spiritually anemic) or dissociates upward (ungrounded highs, sleep disturbance, brittle certainty). The remedy is not "more light," but truer light that lands.

MODERN EXPOSURES THAT FRAY THE CROWN
1) Spectacle, Branding, and "Spiritual Theater"

When devotion becomes content and practice becomes performance, sincerity thins. The crown learns that presence must be impressive to be valid.
Medicine: do one practice no one sees—small, hidden, daily.

2) Information Without Initiation

Endless teachings, few transformations. Concepts pile up where consecration should live.
Medicine: choose one lineage/ritual for a season; let depth replace novelty.

3) Polarization & Manufactured Outrage

Contempt is sand in the chalice. Chronic us-vs-them collapses the sense of shared spirit.
Medicine: guard your hour of unopinionated silence. Practice blessing those you disagree with.

4) Light Pollution & Broken Rhythm

Nights that never darken blunt the body's capacity for hush and wonder.
Medicine: end the day by candle/low light; greet one natural light daily (dawn, dusk, moon).

5) Predatory Authority & Cultic Dynamics

When leaders demand surrender without safeguarding dignity, the crown's trust in benevolence fractures.
Medicine: sovereignty clauses—consent, questions welcome, exits honored. Measure "truth" by fruits: humility, service, mercy.

6) Nihilism & the Commerce of Despair

A culture that monetizes doom teaches the nervous system that meaning is naïve.
Medicine: micro-awe—stars for 60 seconds, a leaf's veins, a child's breath. Small doors open the great room.

PSYCHIC POLLUTION AT THE CROWN

Thoughtforms heavy with contempt, superiority, and hopelessness haze the halo. In such atmospheres, people feel: "What's the point?" or "I must transcend to escape." Both sever communion.
Cleansing image: a soft, luminous rain falling through the

crown, pooling warm at the heart, then flowing down the spine into the feet—light that descends and roots.

EMOTIONAL TOXINS THAT DIM THE HALO

- Shame (I am disqualified from grace).
- Spiritual unworthiness (I must earn belonging).
- Grief without witness (loss that never met the altar).
  These teach the psyche to brace against benediction. The crown cannot open where the heart cannot weep.
  Practice: name one sorrow aloud daily; place it on a simple altar; whisper, *"Belong."*

COLLECTIVE DESENSITIZATION

When a society derides reverence and replaces ritual with consumption, the communal crown contracts, yet the grid re-opens through ordinary sanctity multiplied: meals blessed, elders honored, work offered, silence shared. Each honest act brightens the field.

VIOLATION OF BELONGING (GASLIGHTING OF SPIRIT)

To be told "your devotion is delusion," "your peace is avoidance," or "your God is wrong" can sever trust in the most intimate bond we know. After such a violation, souls often oscillate between numbness and frenzied seeking.
Restoration: reintroduce safe Presence—gentle rituals, non-coercive community, quiet prayers that ask for nothing: *"Be with me."* Let devotion be friendship again.

SIGNS OF CROWN IMBALANCE

- Underactive: spiritual flatness, meaning-crisis, isolation in crowds, dryness in prayer/meditation.

- Overactive/ungrounded: dissociation, sleep disturbance, escapist "transcendence," dogmatic certainty, bypassing pain.
- Body whispers: vertex tension, light sensitivity at night, feel "top-heavy," difficulty *receiving* comfort.

PURIFYING THE CROWN: PRACTICES THAT RE-SANCTIFY

Hygiene of Silence

- 10 minutes daily of wordless sitting. No mantra, no goal; simply *be*.
- Weekly hour of tech-Sabbath; end it by stepping outside and looking up.

Descent of Light (very important)

- After any prayer/meditation, trace awareness: crown → brow → throat → heart → belly → feet.
- Say, *"Let the light I receive become the love I give."*

Liturgy of the Ordinary

- Choose one act as daily sacrament: making tea, folding cloth, watering plants. Do it slowly, gratefully.

Rituals of Belonging

- Bless your thresholds (door, bed, desk) with a touch and a word: *"This is holy ground."*
- Eat one meal in mindful silence; dedicate it to someone in need.

Awe & Earth

- Moon-watch, sunrise breath, bare feet on soil. Let cosmos and soil meet in you.

Community & Service

- Sing with others. Serve once a week in a way that costs a little comfort and returns much meaning.

Discernment

- Before adopting any teaching, ask:
    1. Does it widen compassion?
    2. Does it honor consent?
    3. Does it help light descend into daily life?

Affirmations

- *I am held in a living Whole.*
- *I let grace descend through me into the world.*
- *Belonging is my native light.*

THE DEEPER LESSON

Sahasrara's toxin is forgetfulness; its antidote is remembrance made ordinary. Not a peak, but a posture. Not escape, but arrival.

You are not required to climb to heaven.
You are invited to let heaven fall like quiet rain,
soaking your words, your work, your resting, until one simple day shimmers like a thousand petals.

Chapter 6 – Signs of Balance

Grace, Unity, and Living Communion (Sahasrara)

When the Crown Chakra (Sahasrara) is balanced, life itself becomes prayer.
Awareness rests in effortless harmony — the mind quiet, the heart radiant, and the spirit at peace.
You no longer seek the Divine as something beyond you; you *remember* it as the essence within and around all things.
Separation dissolves. Every breath feels sacred, every act imbued with meaning.

A balanced Sahasrara does not escape the world — it embraces it.
It is the marriage of heaven and earth, transcendence and embodiment, silence and song.
Through this union, wisdom ripens into compassion, and knowledge flowers into love.

INNER PEACE AND LIVING STILLNESS

When Sahasrara is open and aligned, stillness no longer feels like absence — it feels like home.
The mind no longer strives to understand everything; it simply allows truth to reveal itself.
Moments unfold without resistance. Awareness expands gently

in all directions, embracing what is without needing to fix or change it.

There is calm certainty beneath uncertainty, serenity beneath activity.
Even amidst chaos, you remain centered in the silent presence that witnesses all.
This is not detachment but deep participation — being so fully present that control becomes unnecessary.

Peace is no longer a goal; it is your natural atmosphere.

DIVINE CONNECTION AND SPIRITUAL UNITY

The hallmark of a balanced Crown Chakra is direct communion — an unbroken awareness of your unity with Source.
This connection transcends belief systems or doctrines; it is an intimate knowing that you are part of a living Whole.
You sense the Divine not as an external being, but as the current flowing through your breath, your touch, your existence.

Moments of synchronicity multiply. Guidance arrives as quiet intuition rather than dramatic revelation.
Prayer becomes less about asking and more about *listening.*
Meditation becomes not an escape from life but a merging *with* it.
Every heartbeat echoes the rhythm of the cosmos.

The balanced Crown whispers: *"You were never apart. You only forgot."*

CLARITY, FAITH, AND TRUST IN LIFE

Sahasrara in harmony bestows unwavering faith — not blind belief, but luminous trust.
You recognize the invisible order behind apparent chaos.

Even life's challenges become teachers, guiding you deeper into wisdom and surrender.

This trust dissolves anxiety about outcomes; you know life unfolds with intelligence beyond the mind's reach.
Fear loosens its grip. Hope becomes confidence, and faith becomes quiet joy.
Gratitude becomes your daily prayer — not for what you receive, but for the miracle of simply being.

HARMONY BETWEEN HEAVEN AND EARTH

A healthy Crown is rooted as much as it is radiant.
You can feel the vastness of Spirit and still delight in the human world — laughter, love, touch, creation.
You no longer see a divide between spiritual and physical life; both are expressions of one consciousness.

Light flows freely through all chakras, descending as inspiration, ascending as devotion.
This exchange creates coherence — your thoughts align with your heart, your words with your purpose, your actions with love.

In this balance, enlightenment is not escape; it is embodiment.

SELF-REALIZATION AND THE DISSOLUTION OF EGO

When Sahasrara is balanced, identity softens from "I" to "I Am."
You recognize that consciousness is not *yours* — it *is you.*
The small self yields to the greater Self — a boundless awareness expressing through form.
Ego becomes a servant of love, no longer the ruler of perception.

You act not from fear of loss or need for control, but from inspiration, compassion, and clarity.
In relationships, this brings humility, forgiveness, and genuine presence.
In solitude, it brings contentment and joy.

This is the freedom of the Crown — not escape from personality, but liberation from its limits.

LUCIDITY OF THOUGHT AND PURE AWARENESS

Balanced Sahasrara refines perception into lucidity — a mental atmosphere clear as mountain air.
Ideas flow easily, creativity feels guided, and insight appears spontaneously in silence.
Your thinking becomes intuitive and spacious, not crowded or forced.

Wisdom feels embodied rather than intellectual; truth arrives as vibration before it becomes words.
You no longer analyze life — you *understand* it through resonance.

Thought becomes light, and light becomes knowing.

PHYSICAL AND ENERGETIC HARMONY

Because Sahasrara interfaces with the brain, pineal gland, and nervous system, balance manifests as radiant vitality and deep rest.
Sleep becomes rejuvenating; waking feels inspired.
The body feels simultaneously lighter and stronger — energized yet serene.
You sense subtle energy currents flowing harmoniously from the root to the crown, uniting the entire chakra system in rhythmic balance.

The aura around the head may feel luminous, tinged with violet or white light — an energetic halo of serenity and grace.
This glow is not seen by all but felt by many — the quiet magnetism of presence itself.

SERVICE, COMPASSION, AND THE JOY OF GIVING

The true sign of Crown activation is not transcendence, but service.
Your devotion turns outward, naturally expressing as kindness, creativity, and contribution.
You no longer seek to be special — you long to be useful.
Acts of compassion arise not from obligation but from recognition:
There is no other.

This understanding transforms relationships, communities, and even the planet.
The desire to heal the world is no longer driven by guilt or pride, but by love recognizing itself.

LIVING IN GRACE

A balanced Crown radiates grace — not as a mystical state, but as ordinary holiness.
You walk slower, breathe deeper, and see beauty in imperfection.
Synchronicities unfold gently, aligning your path without struggle.
You feel guided, yet free; inspired, yet grounded.

You no longer pray for light — you *become* it.
You no longer search for meaning — you *embody* it.

The enlightened state is not elsewhere.
It is this moment, lived in awareness, where heaven and earth meet as you.

THE DEEPER LESSON

Sahasrara teaches that illumination is not ascent, but arrival.
When the Crown is balanced, you cease striving for awakening
— because you are already awake.
You remember that consciousness does not need to improve
itself; it only needs to express itself fully through your life.

To live with an open Crown is to walk as a bridge between
worlds — mind clear, heart open, body grounded, soul free.

You are the thousand-petaled lotus — not reaching for the light,
but *unfolding because of it.*

The Feeling of Divine Illumination

Crown Chakra (Sahasrara)

When the Crown Chakra is balanced, life feels like light
remembering itself.
There is no struggle between body and spirit, self and Source,
thought and silence.
Awareness expands yet remains intimate — infinite
consciousness touching the smallest breath.
You no longer reach upward; you *open inward*, and the universe
blooms where you stand.

The feeling of clear sight at the Crown is not vision — it is
knowing through being.
There is no effort to perceive truth, for truth is what you are.
The veil between seeker and sought dissolves.
Understanding does not arrive through thought but through
radiance — through the simple, wordless recognition that
everything is holy.

THE ELEMENT OF CONSCIOUSNESS: PURE LIGHT BEYOND LIGHT

While the Third Eye refines vision through the element of light, Sahasrara transcends even that — it is Light itself, before color or form.
This is not the light that shines upon things, but the luminous field in which all things exist.
It cannot be seen, only *realized.*

When balanced, this light does not blind or overwhelm; it softens perception into unity.
You no longer look *at* the world but *as* the world — consciousness seeing itself reflected in every detail.
This is the flowering of awareness, where light and love are no longer separate vibrations but the same frequency of existence.

Sahasrara whispers: "You are not the one who sees the light — you are the light that sees."

THE FEELING OF LUMINOUS STILLNESS

The peace of the Crown is vast yet tender — a stillness that vibrates with life.
Time feels fluid; breath feels infinite.
There is no rush to arrive, no fear of ending.
Your mind floats in quiet wonder, not empty but radiant with meaning.
Every sound carries silence within it; every silence hums with creation.

In this state, you sense that consciousness itself breathes through you.
There is no boundary between meditation and living, no gap between sacred and ordinary.
Stillness becomes movement, and movement becomes prayer.

THE BIOENERGETICS OF UNITY

Sahasrara anchors its radiance through the pineal gland, cerebral cortex, and the crown of the head — the gateway where subtle energy transitions into pure awareness.
When harmonized, these centers pulse with delicate rhythm — not excitement, but coherence.
The nervous system relaxes into order; brain waves slow into serenity; hormones align with natural cycles of light and dark.
You feel bright yet rested, present yet infinite.

The entire body becomes an antenna of consciousness — grounded through the Root, luminous through the Crown, vibrating as one integrated field.
Every cell becomes aware of its place in the cosmic design.

The nervous system no longer reacts; it receives.

THE EXPERIENCE OF DIVINE UNION

The most profound sign of balance in Sahasrara is the felt sense of oneness.
It cannot be taught, only remembered.
You feel connected to all beings without effort — compassion flows naturally, forgiveness arises spontaneously, and gratitude becomes breath itself.
There is no hierarchy in awareness: the ant, the mountain, and the star are facets of the same jewel.

This union does not erase individuality; it transfigures it.
Your uniqueness becomes the instrument through which the Divine sings.
You realize that enlightenment is not the rejection of humanity, but its sanctification.

THE BRIDGE OF HEAVEN AND EARTH

When Sahasrara radiates clearly, energy circulates freely
through all chakras.
Spirit descends as inspiration, body rises as devotion —
meeting in the heart as living wisdom.
You no longer climb toward heaven; you *become the meeting
point* where heaven enters the world.
Ideas, art, and service flow through you like a clear river of
grace.

The mind remains bright but humble — not seeking to control
meaning, only to express it.
Love guides thought, and thought gives voice to love.
This is the "circuit of illumination," where all levels of being —
physical, emotional, mental, and spiritual — act in harmony as
one consciousness.

THE INNER ATMOSPHERE OF THE BALANCED
CROWN

- Emotionally: Profound serenity, awe, and devotion
  replace anxiety or striving.
- Mentally: Thoughts arise as clarity, not commentary.
  Inspiration feels received, not manufactured.
- Physically: Head and scalp feel light, eyes soft, breath
  slow, posture naturally upright.
- Energetically: A subtle pulse or glow at the top of the
  head — the lotus of light unfolding petal by petal.
- Spiritually: Direct knowing that the Divine is not
  elsewhere — it is the awareness reading these words.

THE FLOW OF CONSCIOUSNESS THROUGH LIGHT

Imagine light descending from infinite space, entering the crown as a waterfall of brilliance, then flowing gently down through every chakra.
With each breath, it saturates the heart, steadies the belly, roots into the earth.
When it rises again, it carries the fragrance of humanity —
compassion, creativity, love — back into the infinite.
This is the eternal rhythm of Sahasrara: illumination and incarnation, ascension and return.

To live with a balanced Crown is to let this rhythm move through you continuously — light becoming love, love becoming life.

THE FEELING OF KNOWING WITHOUT THOUGHT

In Sahasrara's stillness, you no longer think truth — you *recognize* it.
Insight arrives as direct experience: tears of understanding, laughter without reason, sudden peace that feels like coming home.
You understand that awakening was never about reaching a summit, but about removing the illusion that there was anywhere else to be.

Awareness does not climb; it unfolds.
Wisdom does not accumulate; it shines.

THE DEEPER LESSON

The Crown Chakra teaches that consciousness is both the
question and the answer, both the seeker and the sought.
When balanced, you cease searching for enlightenment because
you realize you are the space it happens in.
Every breath becomes revelation; every moment, meditation.

You walk gently, not because you fear breaking something
sacred, but because you know everything is.
This is the feeling of divine illumination —
the still joy of being awake,
the serenity of seeing through God's eyes,
and the quiet wonder of knowing
that you were never separate from the light you sought.

Chapter 7 – Hidden Secrets & Esoteric Wisdom

Tantra and the Crown Chakra (Sahasrara)

THE LOTUS OF A THOUSAND SUNS

In Tantric cosmology, Sahasrara is the thousand-petaled lotus — the radiant seat of enlightenment where consciousness recognizes itself as infinite. It is not a chakra in the traditional sense but the flowering of all chakras united. Where Ajna perceives light, Sahasrara becomes it.

Here, Kundalini Shakti completes her ascent, merging with Shiva, pure awareness. Their union dissolves the final illusion of separation — the dance of subject and object, seeker and sought, ends in still radiance.

This is the crown of realization, where perception yields to presence and knowledge transforms into *knowingness* itself.

"There is no longer an I that sees God — there is only God seeing through I."

THE DESCENT OF LIGHT: THE RETURN OF SHAKTI

Tantric texts teach that when Shakti rises and merges with Shiva at Sahasrara, she does not remain there. Her radiance — now divine awareness — descends once more, sanctifying the body and world.

This descent is called Amrita, the nectar of immortality, flowing down through the crown into every cell, anointing creation with consciousness.
Thus, enlightenment is not escape but embodiment — the Divine made visible through human life.

The adept no longer ascends to reach the Divine; the Divine flows through the adept.
Light no longer seeks; it gives.
Awareness no longer climbs; it descends as grace.

THE GREAT MARRIAGE: SHIVA AND SHAKTI AS ONE

In Ajna, Shakti shines as light, and Shiva perceives as awareness.
In Sahasrara, there is no longer two — no dance, no dialogue, only still union.
Shiva's infinite silence and Shakti's radiant energy dissolve into the same vibrationless brilliance — the field of pure consciousness (*Param Jyoti*).

This is the final alchemy of Tantra:

- Sound becomes silence.
- Light becomes awareness.
- Awareness becomes love.
- Love becomes everything.

In this state, there is no practice left to perform, no mantra to chant, no vision to behold — for *you* are the mantra, the vision, the truth realized.

"At the crown, the lover and the beloved are one — awareness resting as eternity."

THE ELEMENT BEYOND ELEMENTS: CONSCIOUSNESS ITSELF

All previous chakras are governed by an element — earth, water, fire, air, ether, light.
Sahasrara transcends them all.
Its element is Chit — *pure consciousness*.
It is the field from which all elements arise and to which they return.

In meditation upon this center, the practitioner may experience infinite vastness, radiant white or violet light, or the gentle hum of cosmic silence (*Anahata Nada*). Yet these are merely thresholds.
The true Sahasrara is formless awareness — the witness before light and sound.

THE THOUSAND-PETALED LOTUS: THE SYMBOL OF INFINITE PERCEPTION

The crown lotus is said to contain a thousand petals — not as number but as metaphor for infinite expression.
Each petal represents a frequency of consciousness, a potential within the cosmic mind.
When awakened, these petals unfurl as understanding — each revelation a petal of the infinite blooming within you.

Unlike other chakras, Sahasrara has no animal guardian — for it transcends instinct and form.
Its living emblem is the White or Thousand-Petaled Lotus, symbol of purity, illumination, and the return to Source.
Just as the lotus rises from muddy waters unstained, consciousness at Sahasrara shines untouched by illusion — radiant in its own perfection.

"The lotus blooms not toward heaven, but from it."

THE NECTAR OF IMMORTALITY (AMRITA)

When the crown opens, the ancient texts say, a subtle nectar drips from the bindu above the head — the *Amrita*, or divine ambrosia.
It cools the fire of desire, heals the body, and bestows serenity.
This nectar is not physical but energetic — the bliss of realization descending through the nervous system as luminous calm.
It nourishes all chakras below, ensuring that enlightenment is lived, not left at the summit.

The practitioner who allows this descent lives in continual blessing — the *Sahasrara state*, where joy does not fluctuate with circumstance but remains as the background music of existence.

KUNDALINI'S FINAL TRANSFORMATION

At the Crown, Kundalini completes her long pilgrimage.
No longer serpent, flame, or current, she becomes light without vibration — pure awareness.
Her dance ceases, but her presence expands.
In her merging with Shiva, time stops — past and future collapse into eternal now.

Then, as grace, she flows downward once more — not as effort, but as blessing, awakening every cell as a living temple of consciousness.
This cycle of ascent and descent — the eternal rhythm of union — is the heartbeat of enlightenment.

TANTRIC PRACTICES FOR SAHASRARA

1. Silent Meditation (Param Shanti):
Sit in complete stillness. Let attention rest in the crown or just above it.
Do not visualize — simply *be*.
When thought arises, see it as ripples within an infinite sky of awareness.

2. Sahasrara Mudra (Lotus of Light):
Hands open above the head, palms facing upward.
Imagine light descending through the crown as you inhale; feel it expand through the heart as you exhale.

3. Breath of Unity (Soham Pranayama):
Inhale silently the sound *So* ("I am That"), exhale *Ham* ("That I am").
Let breath and awareness merge until the mantra disappears into stillness.

4. Meditation on the Thousand-Petaled Lotus:
Visualize a vast lotus opening above your head, petals shimmering with white-gold light.
At its center, a point of brilliant radiance — the source of all creation.
Allow your consciousness to merge into that point, dissolving boundaries of identity.

SIGNS OF CROWN ACTIVATION

- Waves of bliss or peace cascading through the body
- Tingling or warmth at the top of the head
- Periods of spontaneous silence or timelessness
- Heightened intuition and compassion
- Dissolution of fear of death or separation
- Deep, effortless gratitude for existence itself

- A sense of guidance flowing from within rather than above

These are not goals but byproducts of alignment — indicators that awareness is remembering its own nature.

THE ESOTERIC SECRET OF SAHASRARA

At the highest initiation, Tantra reveals that Sahasrara is not merely at the top of the head — it is everywhere.
The thousand petals expand beyond the body, forming the mandala of existence itself.
Here, there is no longer an *individual* crown — only the Crown of Creation, awareness looking out through infinite forms.

The great mystery is that enlightenment was never gained — it was simply uncovered.
The self that sought illumination was the light all along.

"The lotus at the crown is not a destination but a remembrance — the awakening of the light that has always been."

THE FINAL LESSON OF THE CROWN

To awaken Sahasrara is to transcend the need for awakening.
The seeker dissolves into the sought; the wave recognizes itself as ocean.
The practice, the practitioner, and the goal merge into a single vibrationless being — *Sat-Chit-Ananda*:
Existence. Consciousness. Bliss.

This is the hidden secret of the Crown Chakra — that God is not reached through effort, but revealed through surrender.
You are not a spark of light moving toward the sun; you are the sun, dreaming of being a spark.

"At the thousand-petaled lotus, all journeys end — and the eternal begins."

Tantric Secrets of the Inner Sky

Crown Chakra (Sahasrara)

THE ELEMENT BEYOND LIGHT — THE VISION THAT SEES ITSELF

The Crown Chakra, Sahasrara, is the realm *beyond* the element of light — it is pure consciousness, *Chit*, the infinite expanse in which even illumination dissolves into awareness.
If Ajna is the sky of Light (Jyoti), Sahasrara is the space beyond the sky, the lightless radiance from which light itself emerges.
Here, vibration ceases, perception melts, and awareness rests in its own perfection.
It is the silent source of every revelation — where the seer, the seeing, and the seen merge into one boundless field of being.

"Light reveals the world, but consciousness reveals light."

Sahasrara is not illumination but that which allows illumination to exist.
It is the *white fire of transcendence*, radiant yet void, eternal yet ever now.
Where Ajna perceives divine truth, Sahasrara becomes divine truth.
Here, sound, light, and thought dissolve into the pulse of existence itself — the hum before vibration, the stillness before creation.

POWER AS PRESENCE

In the lower centers, power expresses as movement — to act, to express, to perceive.
At Sahasrara, power transforms into Presence.
There is nothing to dominate, no truth to uncover, no path to follow.
Power here is the absolute stillness that *contains* all movement — the cosmic awareness that allows life to unfold through you, without interference.

True mastery of Sahasrara lies not in transcendence *away from life*, but in becoming transparent to it.
You are no longer the observer of creation; you are its conscious unfolding.
Every moment becomes divine self-expression — effortless, luminous, complete.

"When you stop reaching for the light, you realize you were the sun all along."

PURPOSE AS BEING

At the Crown, purpose dissolves into beingness.
The soul no longer seeks meaning through doing or knowing — it *is* meaning itself.
Each breath, each sensation, each thought becomes the play (*Lila*) of divine awareness.
The yogi no longer asks, *"Why am I here?"* — for the question and the answer arise from the same source.

To live from Sahasrara is to realize that creation needs no justification.
Being is purpose.
Awareness is action.
Existence is enlightenment.

THE INNER MARRIAGE — SHIVA AND SHAKTI IN ABSOLUTE UNION

In Ajna, Shiva (awareness) and Shakti (illumination) gaze upon one another — still distinct, though inseparable.
At Sahasrara, their gaze ends. There is no longer duality — no lover and beloved, no dance between knowing and known.
The two currents fuse into one vibrationless expanse — Param Jyoti, the light beyond light, pure being.

This union is not ecstatic motion, but still radiance — the serenity of absolute fulfillment.
Shiva is no longer the witness; Shakti is no longer the energy — both dissolve into Eka Ananda, the One Bliss.
Tantra calls this the Mahasamadhi of Consciousness — the moment creation returns to its origin, the dream folds back into the dreamer.

"In Sahasrara, Shiva and Shakti cease to meet — for there are no two left to unite."

THE THOUSAND-PETALED LOTUS: SYMBOL OF INFINITE PERCEPTION

Sahasrara is described as a thousand-petaled lotus, not for number, but for infinity.
Each petal represents a frequency of consciousness, a vibration of divine expression.
When awakened, these petals unfurl as understanding — every revelation a petal of awakening, every moment a bloom of eternity.

This lotus faces upward, receiving the light of infinity — yet it also radiates downward, blessing every chakra below.
It is both crown and root of the spiritual body — the place where heaven touches earth through awareness.

Unlike other centers, Sahasrara has no animal guardian — it has transcended form.
Its living emblem is the White Lotus, the blossom of liberation that grows from no soil and bends toward no sun — the eternal bloom of being itself.

KUNDALINI'S RETURN AS AMRITA — THE NECTAR OF GRACE

When Kundalini reaches Sahasrara, her ascent is complete.
She dissolves into the brilliance of pure awareness — Shakti merging with Shiva — yet the story does not end.
Her return flow begins as Amrita, the nectar of immortality.
This subtle current, described in the *Tantras* as a cool, luminous stream, descends through the crown to bathe every chakra below.
It is the descent of grace, where enlightenment becomes embodiment.

This nectar awakens the cells, harmonizes the body, and anoints the world as sacred.
It is consciousness remembering itself as creation — heaven flowing into matter.

"At the summit, the serpent does not rest — she becomes the river of light that nourishes the world."

TANTRIC PRACTICES FOR SAHASRARA

1. Silent Union (Param Dhyana):
Sit in stillness, eyes closed, awareness resting just above the crown.
Do not visualize, chant, or concentrate.
Let thought fade into awareness, and awareness expand beyond boundary.
This is meditation without object — the state of pure being.

2. Sahasrara Mudra (Crown Offering):
Raise both hands above the head, palms open to the infinite.
Breathe slowly, feeling each inhale as light descending, each
exhale as peace spreading through the body.

3. The Breath of Bliss (Soham):
Inhale with the inner sound *So* ("I am That"), exhale *Ham*
("That I am").
Let the mantra dissolve into silence until only awareness
remains.

4. White Lotus Visualization:
See a radiant lotus blooming above the head — petals of
translucent white light opening endlessly.
At its center, a point of golden brilliance, radiating through the
crown into infinite space.
Merge awareness with that center until the boundaries between
"I" and "Light" vanish.

SIGNS OF THE CROWN'S AWAKENING

- Pulsing warmth or tingling at the crown or above the
  head
- Waves of bliss, serenity, or timelessness
- Spontaneous stillness or silence within thought
- A sense of unity with all beings
- Dissolution of fear of death or separation
- Natural compassion and effortless forgiveness
- Awareness of life as a single divine rhythm

These are not supernatural gifts, but the ordinary experience of
consciousness when freed from illusion.

THE TANTRIC SECRET OF THE CROWN

The hidden wisdom of Sahasrara is non-duality — that the
witness and the witnessed are one.
Awakening does not occur *through* perception, but *beyond* it.
When the light of Ajna turns upward, it vanishes into infinite
luminosity.
There is no longer vision — only awareness aware of itself.

Tantra teaches that at this stage, the soul becomes the Inner Sky
— boundless, self-luminous, and eternally free.
The yogi who abides here does not leave the world, but blesses
it simply by being.
Their very presence radiates peace — the fragrance of the
thousand-petaled lotus.

"The universe is not outside you.
You are the space in which the universe shines."

THE HIDDEN LESSON — THE LIGHT THAT BECOMES LOVE

The final revelation of Tantra is that consciousness seeks not to
escape form but to love it.
When the light of Sahasrara descends again, it does not
diminish — it multiplies as compassion.
It flows through the heart as forgiveness, through the throat as
truth, through the hands as service, through the eyes as blessing.
This is the true crown — not exaltation, but embodied divinity.

The yogi becomes a living bridge — awareness grounded in
form, heaven expressed as humanity.
There is no more striving, no more seeking — only the natural
radiance of being awake.

THE ULTIMATE TANTRIC TRUTH

At the Crown, enlightenment is not an achievement — it is remembrance.
Nothing new is gained; only illusion falls away.
The final veil reveals that the one who sought God was God, dreaming of separation.

"When the thousand-petaled lotus blooms, there is no light to follow — for you have become the sky it shines within."

This is Sahasrara — the Inner Heaven, the Silence beyond Light, the Infinite returning to Itself.

Overview of the Chakras and Kundalini

The Sacred Architecture of Human Consciousness

In Tantric and Yogic philosophy, the chakras are not merely centers of energy — they are gateways of consciousness, unfolding from the density of matter to the radiance of pure spirit.
They represent the journey of Kundalini Shakti, the divine life force that sleeps at the base of the spine and ascends through the subtle body, awakening each center in turn.
This journey is the alchemy of human evolution — the path from survival to self-realization, from separation to unity, from instinct to divine intelligence.

"The chakras are the steps of a living temple, and Kundalini is the flame that rises through it."

THE SERPENT OF LIGHT: KUNDALINI SHAKTI

Kundalini is the coiled energy of consciousness — Shakti, the
sacred feminine force that animates creation.
In her dormant state, she rests at the base of the spine, spiraled
three and a half times around the Root Chakra.
When awakened through devotion, breath, sound, or grace, she
begins to ascend the Sushumna Nadi, the central channel of
light that connects all seven chakras.

Her journey is not merely upward — it is transformational.
At each center, she awakens latent potentials: instinct becomes
awareness, emotion becomes love, will becomes purpose, and
vision becomes unity.
When she reaches the Crown Chakra, she merges with Shiva,
pure consciousness, completing the sacred union of energy and
awareness.
From there, her energy descends again, blessing the entire body
with divine illumination — the embodiment of enlightenment.

"When Kundalini awakens, you do not rise above life — life
rises through you."

THE SEVEN PRIMARY CHAKRAS
1. Muladhara — The Root Chakra

Element: Earth
Color: Red
Location: Base of the spine
Mantra: *LAM*
Principle: Survival, grounding, security
Archetype: The Guardian

Muladhara is the foundation — the root of being, the place
where spirit meets matter.
Here, consciousness experiences embodiment — the right to
exist, to belong, and to feel safe.

When balanced, it grants stability, vitality, and trust in life's process.
When awakened by Kundalini, the earth itself seems to pulse through your being — grounding spiritual awareness in physical presence.

"From the earth I rise — steady, strong, and alive."

2. Svadhisthana — The Sacral Chakra

Element: Water
Color: Orange
Location: Lower abdomen
Mantra: *VAM*
Principle: Pleasure, emotion, creativity
Archetype: The Creator

Svadhisthana is the ocean of emotion — the seat of desire, sensuality, and flow.
Here, consciousness learns movement, adaptability, and the joy of creation.
When balanced, it brings emotional intelligence, healthy sexuality, and creative abundance.
Kundalini stirs this center as waves of vitality and joy — energy becomes fluid, and life begins to dance.

"I flow with the tides of creation — open, alive, and free."

3. Manipura — The Solar Plexus Chakra

Element: Fire
Color: Yellow
Location: Navel region
Mantra: *RAM*
Principle: Power, will, transformation
Archetype: The Warrior

Manipura is the inner sun — the forge of identity, determination, and purpose.
Here, fire refines the raw material of emotion into intention and action.
When balanced, it grants confidence, discipline, and self-mastery.
When Kundalini ignites this fire, it becomes the fuel of transformation — turning fear into courage, doubt into decision, and effort into illumination.

"Through the fire of will, I become the light of purpose."

4. Anahata — The Heart Chakra

Element: Air
Color: Green (or pink)
Location: Center of the chest
Mantra: *YAM*
Principle: Love, compassion, unity
Archetype: The Healer

Anahata is the bridge between body and spirit, the meeting place of human and divine.
Here, love expands beyond emotion — it becomes a state of being.
When balanced, it opens compassion, forgiveness, and the capacity to love without attachment.
Kundalini in the heart manifests as radiant warmth — energy that breathes through every cell, harmonizing all that it touches.

"I am love in motion — breath, balance, and grace."

5. Vishuddha — The Throat Chakra

Element: Ether (Space)
Color: Blue
Location: Throat

Mantra: *HAM*
Principle: Truth, expression, resonance
Archetype: The Messenger

Vishuddha is the resonance of truth — the voice of the soul.
Here, vibration becomes sound, and expression becomes creation.
When balanced, it brings authenticity, integrity, and inspired communication.
Kundalini flows through this chakra as sacred sound — *Nada Brahma*, the music of the universe, vibrating through speech, song, and silence alike.

"I speak the truth of my soul, and it echoes through eternity."

6. Ajna — The Third Eye Chakra

Element: Light
Color: Indigo
Location: Between the eyebrows
Mantra: *OM*
Principle: Perception, intuition, vision
Archetype: The Seer

Ajna is the lamp of insight — the temple where awareness perceives itself.
Here, the mind becomes luminous; thought refines into intuition.
When balanced, perception is clear, and truth shines through illusion.
Kundalini as light awakens this center as radiance — awareness expands beyond time, and the inner and outer worlds merge in vision.

"I see through illusion into the light of truth."

7. Sahasrara — The Crown Chakra

Element: Consciousness (Beyond Form)
Color: White or Violet
Location: Crown of the head / just above it
Mantra: *Silence* (or *OM beyond sound*)
Principle: Unity, enlightenment, divine connection
Archetype: The Mystic

Sahasrara is the thousand-petaled lotus — the crown of illumination where all dualities dissolve.
Here, Kundalini completes her ascent, merging Shakti (energy) with Shiva (awareness).
The mind becomes still, the heart limitless, and the body radiant with divine consciousness.
Enlightenment is not departure but embodiment — the realization that all creation is sacred and all life is one.

"I am not the drop in the ocean — I am the ocean remembering itself as a drop."

The Journey of Ascent and Descent

THE ASCENT — FROM MATTER TO SPIRIT

Kundalini's rise through the chakras is the evolution of consciousness:

- From survival to surrender
- From instinct to intuition
- From earth to infinity

Each chakra represents a passage — grounding, emotion, will, love, truth, vision, unity — refining the human into the divine.

THE DESCENT — FROM SPIRIT TO MATTER

But true mastery begins when the energy flows downward again.
After merging with Shiva at the Crown, Kundalini descends as Amrita, the nectar of grace.
This descent sanctifies the physical world — bringing spirit into body, heaven into earth, consciousness into creation.
The awakened being lives in both realms — anchored in form, aware of formlessness.

"The serpent rises for realization, and returns for embodiment."

THE ETERNAL DANCE OF SHIVA AND SHAKTI

Throughout this sacred architecture, two forces move as one:

- Shiva, the unmoving awareness — eternal, infinite, pure.
- Shakti, the dynamic energy — creative, loving, alive.

Their union is the pulse of existence — the dance of light and life, stillness and movement, heaven and earth.
Through their interplay, consciousness becomes creation, and creation remembers consciousness.

"When Shiva dreams, worlds are born.
When Shakti awakens, they return to light."

THE LIVING TEMPLE WITHIN

The chakras are not distant heavens but living gates within the human form.
Each breath, emotion, and thought is an expression of their energy.
When they align, life becomes a harmonious current — a divine symphony of matter and spirit.
Through awareness, love, and practice, you become both the

instrument and the music — the awakened embodiment of the cosmic song.

"The chakras are not climbed but revealed — for you were never separate from the light they contain."

How to Awaken Each Chakra

The Practice of Living Light

Each chakra responds to both intention and embodiment — not forced activation, but conscious alignment.
Awakening is not a single event; it is a rhythm of remembrance, breath by breath.
Kundalini does not rise through effort, but through readiness.
When energy flows freely from the Root to the Crown, the soul begins to hum in harmony with creation — a living current of divine intelligence moving through matter.

Below is a practical yet sacred method to awaken each center in sequence.
These practices can be done individually or as a daily full-body meditation.

1. Root Chakra (Muladhara) — Grounding the Light

Purpose: Stability, security, embodiment.
Element: Earth   Color: Red   Mantra: *LAM*

How to Awaken:

1. Posture of Earth: Sit cross-legged or stand barefoot. Feel the soles of your feet or the base of your spine connect to the ground.

2. Breath of Grounding: Inhale deeply, imagining drawing energy from the earth into your pelvis. Exhale, releasing fear and instability.
3. Visualization: See a red sphere glowing at the base of your spine — dense, warm, steady. With each breath, it grows stronger, anchoring you in safety.
4. Affirmation: "I am safe. I belong. Life supports me."
5. Embodiment Practice: Walk slowly and mindfully, noticing each step. Eat grounding foods (root vegetables, proteins). Engage in simple physical labor — tending, carrying, building.
6. Awakening Cue: A feeling of heaviness releases; you feel rooted, calm, and supported by existence itself.

2. Sacral Chakra (Svadhisthana) — Flowing with Emotion

Purpose: Creativity, sensuality, emotional expression.
Element: Water   Color: Orange   Mantra: *VAM*

How to Awaken:

1. Breath of Flow: Inhale into the belly, exhale through the hips. Let your abdomen move freely.
2. Movement: Gentle hip circles or flowing dance awaken this water element. Allow motion to dissolve stagnation.
3. Visualization: Imagine orange light swirling in your lower abdomen — liquid, luminous, fluid.
4. Affirmation: "I flow with life. My emotions move through me with grace."
5. Aromatherapy: Use ylang-ylang, sandalwood, or orange oil to soften emotional resistance.
6. Creative Expression: Write, paint, sing, or cook intuitively — creation is the movement of Shakti through form.
7. Awakening Cue: You feel lighter, joyful, emotionally expressive, connected to pleasure and play.

3. Solar Plexus Chakra (Manipura) — Igniting the Fire of Will

Purpose: Confidence, strength, transformation.
Element: Fire   Color: Yellow   Mantra: *RAM*

How to Awaken:

1. Breath of Power (Kapalabhati): Short, rhythmic exhales through the nose, activating the navel center.
2. Posture of Power: Sit tall or stand in Warrior Pose; feel the spine strong, the belly alive.
3. Visualization: See a golden sun in your abdomen, radiating warmth outward.
4. Affirmation: "I act with purpose. I transform challenges into light."
5. Journaling Practice: Write down one fear and one courageous action. Take that action mindfully.
6. Dietary Balance: Warm foods, ginger, turmeric, and moderate fasting support Manipura's fire.
7. Awakening Cue: You feel decisive, energized, and luminous — fear replaced by inner strength.

4. Heart Chakra (Anahata) — Expanding into Love

Purpose: Compassion, forgiveness, unity.
Element: Air   Color: Green (or pink)   Mantra: *YAM*

How to Awaken:

1. Breath of Love: Inhale deeply into your heart, exhale softly, imagining your breath expanding in all directions.
2. Visualization: A glowing emerald or rose light blossoms in the center of your chest, radiating warmth and acceptance.
3. Affirmation: "I am love. I forgive and am forgiven."

4. Sound: Chant *YAM* slowly, letting the vibration resonate through the sternum.
5. Service: Offer one small act of kindness each day without expectation.
6. Reflection Practice: Place your hands on your heart and think of someone you love — then someone who challenges you — sending love to both equally.
7. Awakening Cue: Emotional heaviness lifts; tears may flow. Peace and gratitude arise spontaneously.

5. Throat Chakra (Vishuddha) — Speaking the Truth of the Soul

Purpose: Communication, authenticity, resonance.
Element: Ether   Color: Blue   Mantra: *HAM*

How to Awaken:

1. Breath of Sound: Inhale through the nose, exhale with a soft humming tone. Feel the vibration in your throat.
2. Visualization: A bright sapphire light spins at the throat, expanding with every breath.
3. Affirmation: "I speak my truth clearly and with love."
4. Creative Practice: Sing, chant, or recite poetry aloud. Voice is vibration — vibration is creation.
5. Integrity Check: Reflect — are there unspoken truths or words said without authenticity? Bring alignment between inner truth and outer expression.
6. Hydration Ritual: Drink water mindfully, blessing it before each sip. Ether flows best through purity and resonance.
7. Awakening Cue: The throat feels open, the voice steady and true. Communication flows effortlessly.

6. Third Eye Chakra (Ajna) — Awakening Inner Vision

Purpose: Intuition, perception, wisdom.
Element: Light   Color: Indigo   Mantra: *OM*

How to Awaken:

1. Trataka (Candle Gazing): Gaze gently at a flame; when eyes tire, close them and observe the inner light.
2. Breath of Clarity: Inhale awareness between the eyebrows; exhale through the temples.
3. Visualization: A radiant indigo orb pulsates in the center of your forehead — clear, steady, infinite.
4. Affirmation: "I see clearly. I trust my intuition."
5. Meditation: Sit in silence, observing thoughts as clouds in the sky. Awareness remains the still witness.
6. Crystals: Use amethyst or lapis lazuli on the brow during meditation.
7. Awakening Cue: Subtle flashes of insight, vivid dreams, intuitive knowing, inner calm.

7. Crown Chakra (Sahasrara) — Uniting with Divine Consciousness

Purpose: Spiritual connection, transcendence, oneness.
Element: Pure Consciousness   Color: White or Violet
Mantra: *Silent OM*

How to Awaken:

1. Meditation on the Inner Sky: Sit with eyes closed, attention slightly above the crown. Feel vastness — no edges, no effort.
2. Breath of Stillness: Inhale light through the crown, exhale awareness through the heart.
3. Visualization: A thousand-petaled white lotus opens, radiating subtle light upward and downward.

4. Affirmation: "I am infinite consciousness, one with all creation."
5. Silence Practice: Allow gaps between thoughts to expand. Rest in the awareness that perceives them.
6. Surrender Ritual: Each night, release the day's identity — whisper, "I am that which witnesses."
7. Awakening Cue: Profound peace, unity, timelessness. No effort to hold presence — you *are* presence.

Integrating the Whole System — The Flow of Kundalini

When all chakras are harmonized, Kundalini flows like a river of light — from root to crown and back again.
To sustain awakening:

- Meditate daily, alternating between grounding and expansion.
- Keep the heart as the bridge, for love balances power and perception.
- Move, breathe, and create — energy in motion stays alive.
- Serve others — compassion keeps the current pure.
- Rest often in silence — awareness is the temple where all elements unite.

"The path of awakening is not climbing upward but remembering inward — discovering that every chakra is a doorway to the same Divine Light."

Western Mysticism: The Light of Creation and the Temple of Divine Illumination

Crown Chakra (Sahasrara)

In Western mysticism, Sahasrara is the Temple of Divine Illumination — the sphere where creation returns to Creator, and light dissolves into the Infinite Mind that birthed it.
If the Third Eye perceives divine light through form, the Crown *becomes* that light — the radiant knowing through which Spirit beholds itself without reflection or veil.
Here, awareness transcends symbol, language, and sight. It is the *Lux Aeterna* — the Eternal Light that is not seen, but *is seeing itself.*

"And there shall be no night there; for the Lord God giveth them light." — *Revelation 22:5*

At this summit of consciousness, illumination is no longer revelation — it is realization.
It is not the mind knowing truth, but truth awakening within itself.
The seeker becomes the sanctuary; the soul becomes the shining presence of the divine.

THE FIRST LIGHT AND THE LAST

In Genesis, the first act of creation was light — the Word made visible.
But in Revelation, that light returns to its source:
"I am Alpha and Omega, the beginning and the end."
Between these two lights unfolds the entire journey of the soul — the descent of consciousness into matter and its return through awareness.
Sahasrara is the Omega of creation — the crown where the light

that once shone *outward* turns *inward*, revealing that there was never separation between Creator and creation.

In this realization, the mystic understands that enlightenment is not the gaining of knowledge, but the remembrance of origin. All form, all experience, all shadow are revealed as movements of divine radiance — one light refracting through infinite prisms of existence.

"God is Light, and in Him is no darkness at all." — *1 John 1:5*

THE TEMPLE ABOVE THE MIND

Where the Third Eye opens the *Cathedral of Vision*, the Crown unfolds the Temple Above the Mind — a sanctum not built of walls or ideas, but of pure being.
It is the Holy of Holies within the human soul — the innermost chamber of divine awareness, where the presence of God is not worshiped as other, but known as Self.

The Christian mystic Meister Eckhart called this place *"the silent desert of Godhead,"* where even the soul ceases to exist as a separate being and melts into the eternal Light.
In Kabbalah, this corresponds to *Keter*, the crown of the Tree of Life — the ineffable brilliance from which all emanations arise. Keter is the source beyond understanding — *Ain Soph Aur*, the Limitless Light, before even thought or creation.

At this level, prayer ends, meditation dissolves, and only awareness remains.
To "enter the Crown" is to pass beyond the veil of all opposites — good and evil, heaven and earth, light and darkness — and to awaken as the still point from which they all emerge.

THE MYSTICAL LIGHT OF UNION

Western mystics spoke of this illumination as the *Uncreated Light* — a radiance not of sun or flame, but of divine essence. It is the same light that transfigured Christ on Mount Tabor, bathed St. Francis in ecstasy, and filled the hearts of the Desert Fathers with wordless peace.

The Hesychasts of the Eastern Church sought this through the *Prayer of the Heart*:
"Lord Jesus Christ, Son of God, have mercy on me."
Repeated until sound vanished into silence, this prayer carried the seeker beyond the senses into the luminous stillness of God's presence.
In that stillness, they reported seeing the "Taboric Light" — not as vision, but as awareness shining through all things.

This is the essence of Sahasrara:
The realization that the light you once beheld as divine now shines as your very consciousness.
There is no longer "God and me" — there is only Light, aware of itself.

THE ALCHEMY OF ASCENT AND RETURN

In the Western Hermetic tradition, the crown corresponds to the completion of the Great Work — the *coniunctio*, or sacred marriage, of Sol and Luna, Spirit and Matter, Shiva and Shakti. Here, the alchemist's fire becomes white — no longer purifying, but illuminating.
All opposites fuse into one radiant field of unity.

This is the "Philosopher's Stone" not as substance, but as *state* — the mind turned to light, the body transfigured into Spirit.
The Hermetic axiom declares:

"That which is above is like unto that which is below."

Sahasrara fulfills this mystery.
The heavens above the crown are reflected in the awareness within.
The divine is no longer sought in the stars or scriptures, but in the stillness of consciousness itself.

THE CHRISTIC CROWN

In the Christian mystery, the "Crown of Thorns" worn by Christ is also the *Crown of Illumination.*
The thorns, piercing the head, symbolize the dissolution of the egoic mind — the surrender of the personal will to divine will.
Through suffering, illusion is pierced, and consciousness expands beyond self.
At resurrection, the thorns become a radiant halo — the transmutation of pain into light, matter into grace.

Thus, Sahasrara is both cross and resurrection, crucifixion and ascension — the moment when human consciousness is lifted into divine realization.
It is the Christ within, forever saying:

"I and my Father are one." — *John 10:30*

THE LIGHT THAT REMAINS

In the final revelation, the mystic sees that light has never departed from its source.
Every ray that ever shone through creation was the Infinite remembering itself.
The seeker's journey — through the chakras, through lifetimes, through all striving — ends where it began: in the eternal radiance of awareness.

At Sahasrara, the soul becomes the flame that no wind can extinguish — consciousness unbound, love without object, light without shadow.

This is the meaning of divine union: not escape from the world, but recognition that the world itself is the body of God.

"The Kingdom of Heaven is within you." — *Luke 17:21*

THE WESTERN SECRET OF SAHASRARA

All mystical lineages converge upon this truth:
That illumination is not received, but revealed; not achieved, but remembered.
The light that spoke creation into being is the same light that now awakens within you.
It shines through your eyes, your thoughts, your every breath.
It is not something you possess, but what you are.

To awaken Sahasrara is to become the Light of the World — the silent lamp through which the divine beholds its own creation.
The mystic, the yogi, and the alchemist alike arrive here — in the luminous simplicity of being, where heaven and earth are one continuum of consciousness.

"The light you seek is the light that seeks you.
And when the two meet, there is only Light."

Chapter 8 – Balancing & Healing Practices

Reiki Positions and Energy Protocols for the Crown Chakra (Sahasrara)

The Crown Chakra (Sahasrara) is the luminous gateway between the finite and the infinite — the bridge through which divine consciousness flows into human awareness.
Located at the crown of the head (and extending slightly above it), it governs spiritual connection, enlightenment, transcendence, and the realization of unity with all life.

In Reiki and subtle-energy practice, Sahasrara is treated *last* in the sequence, once all lower chakras have been harmonized. This ensures that the energy of divine illumination has a clear and grounded channel through which to descend — anchoring spiritual light into the body and heart rather than escaping into abstraction.

When balanced, the Crown awakens serenity, devotion, faith, and the quiet joy of being one with existence.
Its healing does not stimulate energy upward; it allows energy to *dissolve upward* — surrendering self into the infinite stillness of Source.

"The thousand-petaled lotus blooms only when all petals of the self have opened to love."

HAND POSITIONS FOR THE CROWN CHAKRA

Because Sahasrara connects to subtle planes beyond the physical body, Reiki touch here is often *hovering* rather than direct.
Let your hands rest in stillness — as if suspended in light — allowing Reiki to flow through rather than from you.
The intention is not to send energy *to* the client, but to open a conduit between their crown and divine intelligence.

Crown Point (Fontanelle or Just Above the Head)

Hold your hands 1–3 inches above the crown of the head.
Imagine your palms filled with radiant white-violet light, descending in a spiral of grace.
This position nourishes the pineal gland and subtle nervous system, aligning the physical body with its divine blueprint.
It restores the original frequency of wholeness — consciousness remembering itself as light.

Halo Sweep

Circle your hands slowly around the crown, tracing an invisible halo.
This balances the left and right energy currents (ida and pingala) as they merge into the central channel (sushumna).
The motion clears static and energetic residue from spiritual overstimulation or scattered mental energy.
Visualize luminous petals opening, one by one, revealing stillness at the center.

Forehead to Crown Integration

Place one hand lightly above the forehead (Third Eye) and the other hovering over the crown.
This connects vision (Ajna) to divine illumination (Sahasrara).
It refines insight into wisdom, allowing intuitive knowing to

rise into universal consciousness.
This position is ideal at the end of advanced healing or
attunement sessions.

Heart to Crown Bridge

Rest one hand over the heart and the other above the crown.
This links love and light, compassion and consciousness —
ensuring that spiritual awakening remains embodied and
compassionate.
Feel the current rising from the heart like golden mist, merging
into white radiance above the head.

ENERGY PROTOCOLS
1. The Violet Flame of Purification

Visualize Reiki flowing as a violet-white spiral of light
descending through the crown.
It clears karmic residue, ancestral imprints, and the subtle cords
that bind awareness to limitation.
Allow this flame to dissolve heaviness or density, transmuting
them into luminous clarity.
Affirm:

"I am purified in the light of divine truth."

This practice cleanses the upper auric layers, releasing mental
fatigue and restoring spiritual vitality.

2. The Descent of Grace

Hold your hands above the head and breathe softly.
Invite Reiki to pour through you like liquid light — not sent,
but received.
Sense this energy cascading down through the central column,
blessing each chakra in turn.
This descent harmonizes the awakened Kundalini energy with

the peace of divine surrender.
You may feel waves of warmth, tingling, or expansion as
awareness settles into luminous stillness.
Affirm:

"Divine light flows through me, balancing heaven and earth
within."

3. The White Lotus Meditation

Rest both hands above the crown, fingers slightly apart.
Visualize a white thousand-petaled lotus slowly unfolding, each
petal shimmering with light.
As Reiki flows, the petals open outward and upward — an
offering to infinity.
When the lotus fully blooms, a golden light radiates downward
through the spine, illuminating every cell.
Remain in silence as the inner and outer worlds merge in perfect
stillness.

4. The Golden Thread Alignment

Using the breath, imagine drawing a golden thread of energy
upward from the base of the spine to the crown.
With each inhalation, awareness rises; with each exhalation,
grace descends.
Your hands remain above the crown, tracing the upward and
downward flow.
This practice unites Shakti (ascending life force) with Shiva
(descending consciousness).
It harmonizes spiritual aspiration with divine embodiment —
enlightenment grounded in the heart of matter.

5. The Breath of Illumination

Inhale light through the crown, exhale peace through the heart.
Continue until breath, light, and awareness feel inseparable.

Now release all visualization and simply *be* the breath — pure presence.
This protocol trains the nervous system to rest in higher frequencies without fatigue, opening the field to sustained illumination.

Affirm:

"I am light, breathing light, within the light of creation."

AFFIRMATIONS FOR SAHASRARA HARMONY

Repeat aloud or in silence:

- "I am one with Divine Consciousness."
- "Light guides every thought, word, and action."
- "I trust the wisdom of the universe unfolding through me."
- "I am peace, I am presence, I am the light eternal."

These affirmations attune the mind to serenity and spiritual coherence. Each repetition reinforces the remembrance of unity.

DAILY PRACTICES OF ILLUMINATION

- Morning: Upon waking, sit upright and visualize a column of light connecting your crown to the infinite above and the earth below. Whisper: *"As above, so below — I am the bridge of light."*
- Daytime: Pause often to feel light streaming through the crown. Let thoughts dissolve into spacious awareness before responding to the world.
- Evening: Before sleep, place a hand above the crown and one over the heart. Invite all experiences of the day to return to Source, transmuted into wisdom and grace.

These simple rituals maintain open flow without overstimulation, ensuring that spiritual awareness supports daily living.

SYMBOLIC SUPPORT
Cho Ku Rei (Power Symbol)

Use above the crown to amplify connection with divine Source. It seals the field, protecting against energetic dispersion after deep meditation.

Sei He Ki (Harmony Symbol)

Balances spiritual insight with emotional compassion. It prevents dissociation or spiritual bypassing by linking Sahasrara's radiance with the heart's empathy.

Hon Sha Ze Sho Nen (Distance Symbol)

Connects the practitioner to the infinite — the timeless dimension of Reiki itself. Use to access higher realms of guidance or during remote spiritual healing work.

Dai Ko Myo (Master Symbol)

The key to enlightenment and divine union. When invoked at the crown, it activates the full radiance of the soul's original light. It aligns personal will with divine will, allowing the practitioner to become a living channel of grace. Affirm:

"Through the great shining light, I am one with all that is."

INTEGRATIVE PRACTICE

- Chant the bija mantra OM, letting it vibrate from the heart through the crown and into the infinite.
- Meditate on white or violet light, visualizing it expanding beyond your body until you dissolve within it.
- Practice Gratitude Awareness — see every being, every circumstance as an expression of divine light.
- Ground illumination by walking barefoot, touching trees, or mindful breathing — spirit embodied in matter.

Through these practices, Sahasrara remains open yet steady, allowing spiritual energy to move through life with grace and clarity.

THE PRACTITIONER'S ROLE

Working with Sahasrara requires humility, devotion, and the willingness to *not do* — to allow Reiki to flow as divine will, not personal intention.
The practitioner becomes transparent, a vessel rather than a force.
Healing arises not from effort but from alignment.

In this state, the practitioner and client merge into one field of awareness.
There is no healer, no healed — only light recognizing itself in another form.
This is the true essence of Crown healing: remembrance of oneness.

"To heal through the Crown is to bless through being."

Sahasrara teaches that enlightenment is not escape from the world — it is illumination within it.
When this chakra is balanced, every thought becomes prayer, every breath communion, every moment grace.
You no longer reach for heaven — you live as its reflection.

"I am the thousand-petaled lotus,
blooming in stillness,
rooted in earth,
open to heaven,
radiant with divine light."

Through this remembrance, the cycle completes — spirit and matter reunited in the eternal dance of light.

Bridging the Heart Chakra to the Crown Chakra

THE PATH OF ASCENSION: FROM LOVE TO ILLUMINATION

The chakras form not a ladder to climb but a spiral of realization—an ascending current through which consciousness remembers its divine origin.
From the steady pulse of the Heart to the infinite radiance of the Crown, energy refines itself from the warmth of love into the brilliance of pure awareness.
Between them flow two luminous gateways: the Throat, which gives the heart its voice, and the Third Eye, which grants vision to the soul.

The journey from Heart to Crown is the journey from devotion to realization, from compassion to communion, from the love

that feels to the light that knows.
At its summit, love and wisdom become indistinguishable; the
soul speaks, sees, and finally *is* the Divine it once sought.

The Golden Bridge of Consciousness

Each of the upper chakras refines vibration into subtler
expressions of Spirit:

- Heart (Anahata): Love, empathy, and sacred connection
  — the pulse of compassion that unites all life.
- Throat (Vishuddha): Resonance and truth — the etheric
  chamber where love becomes sound and wisdom begins
  to move.
- Third Eye (Ajna): Vision and perception — the eye
  through which vibration turns to light, and thought
  becomes understanding.
- Crown (Sahasrara): Illumination and unity — the
  thousand-petaled lotus of divine consciousness where
  sound and light dissolve back into silence.

Through this ascending bridge, the current of the Heart rises
upward, gradually releasing its weight of emotion and density
until it becomes the luminous breath of the Infinite.
The Throat translates the feeling of love into vibration.
The Third Eye translates vibration into insight.
And the Crown receives insight as pure presence — love
remembered as light.

This is the alchemy of ascension: the transformation of
compassion into wisdom, and of wisdom into divine knowing.

The Crown as the Portal of Return

Sahasrara is not merely the highest center—it is the point of
return, where the spiral of consciousness completes its circuit.
All energies refined through the Heart, Throat, and Third Eye

converge here as a single ray, dissolving individuality into universal awareness.
Where the Heart expands outward, the Crown opens upward; where the Throat vibrates, the Crown is still.

It is the meeting of the human and the eternal—the quiet convergence of all prayers into silence.
Through this portal, energy ceases its motion and becomes radiance.
It no longer seeks expression, understanding, or experience.
It simply *is*.

To reach the Crown is not to climb higher but to surrender deeper—to let the current of love ascend and vanish into the brilliance of its source.

The Energetic Continuum: From Compassion to Communion

Each of these upper chakras embodies a sacred affirmation of consciousness unfolding:

- Heart: *I love.*
- Throat: *I express.*
- Third Eye: *I perceive.*
- Crown: *I am.*

Together they form the mantra of realization—the movement from relationship to unity.
When the current flows unhindered, love evolves into wisdom, and wisdom blossoms into illumination.
Every word becomes vibration, every thought becomes light, and every silence becomes God.

When energy reaches the Crown, the journey of the chakras culminates in wholeness.

The separate voices of the inner centers merge into one harmonic tone—the soundless sound of existence.

The Bridge of Light in the Human Temple

The human body is a cathedral of resonance.
The Heart is its sacred altar, the Throat its choir, the Third Eye its stained glass of insight, and the Crown its luminous dome.
When the Heart prays, the Throat sings, the Third Eye envisions, and the Crown receives, the entire temple becomes radiant.

Through this inner architecture, the soul ascends not by effort but by attunement.
Breath rises through the spine as a thread of gold; love transforms into vibration, vibration into illumination, and illumination into pure being.
When all four centers harmonize, a living halo forms around the head—the auric crown of awakened consciousness, radiant with peace.

This is the natural outcome of Reiki, meditation, or prayer practiced with sincerity: the restoration of the human field into coherence with divine order.

The Descent of Light

As energy completes its ascent into the Crown, it immediately begins its descent—a gentle outpouring of grace that flows back through the body.
The light that rose as aspiration now returns as blessing.
It flows through the Third Eye as wisdom, through the Throat as compassion in speech, through the Heart as unconditional love, grounding again into the Earth as embodied service.

Thus, Sahasrara is not the end of the path but its fulfillment and renewal—the constant exchange between heaven and earth

within the human form.
Through this circulation, enlightenment becomes life itself, not a distant state but a living rhythm: love rising as light, light returning as love.

Cross-Cultural Parallels: The Ascent to the Divine

IN YOGIC AND TANTRIC PHILOSOPHY

The Heart represents *Vāyu Tattva* (air)—movement and connection.
The Throat refines this into *Ākāśa Tattva* (ether)—resonance and truth.
The Third Eye becomes *Mahat Tattva*—the luminous field of perception.
At the Crown lies *Pure Consciousness*—the silent unity from which all elements emerge and to which they return.

The yogic journey through these tattvas mirrors the transformation of the soul:
Air becomes ether, ether becomes light, light becomes Spirit.
Here, Sahasrara is the culmination—the disappearance of all vibration into infinite stillness.

IN CHRISTIAN MYSTICISM

The Heart corresponds to the compassion of Christ; the Throat to the Word that reveals it; the Third Eye to divine vision; and the Crown to the Beatific Vision—the soul's direct perception of God.
At the summit, prayer ceases because union is complete.
The soul no longer speaks to the Divine—it *is* the Divine speaking itself into creation.

IN TAOIST ALCHEMY

The Heart holds fire; the Throat refines breath; the Crown radiates light. This upward transformation of *Qi* into *Shen* mirrors the same ascension described in yoga: essence becoming energy, energy becoming spirit. The Taoists call this *Returning to the Source*—the completion of the inner circulation where heaven and earth exist as one continuum.

LIVING THE BRIDGE

To live the bridge from Heart to Crown is to live as resonance itself—to embody the silent language through which love becomes illumination. It is to speak with clarity born of compassion, to see with wisdom born of silence, and to act with presence born of unity.

When the Heart, Throat, Third Eye, and Crown align, your life becomes a prayer in motion:

- Love is your vibration.
- Truth is your voice.
- Insight is your vision.
- Light is your being.

In this realization, nothing needs to be achieved.
Heaven and earth are already meeting in the temple of your awareness. Every heartbeat echoes eternity; every breath bridges worlds.

"Through the open heart, I love.
Through the open crown, I am.
Between them flows the river of light—
The song of God made human."

Western Mysticism and Alchemy: The Marriage of Light and Spirit

THE CROWN AS THE COMPLETION OF THE GREAT WORK

In Western mysticism, the culmination of all transformation was called the Great Work — *Magnum Opus* — the sacred alchemy through which the soul refines itself from matter to Spirit, from love to illumination, from duality to divine unity.
Where the lower mysteries united Earth, Water, Air, and Fire to purify body, emotion, and will, the higher mysteries joined Ether and Light — space and radiance — in the exalted union known as *The Marriage of Light and Spirit.*

This final union completes the ascent of consciousness through the upper chakras:

- Ether (Throat) — Vibration, expression, and resonance.
- Light (Third Eye) — Vision, perception, and revelation.
- Spirit (Crown) — Stillness, unity, and divine realization.

The alchemists taught that just as base metal was transmuted into gold, so perception could be transmuted into truth.
This transformation was not of matter but of mind — not the forging of physical gold, but the awakening of the inner sun, the radiant light of consciousness that outshines all illusion.

In Hermetic philosophy, this stage was called the Illumination of Spiritus Mercurii — when sound becomes light, light becomes wisdom, and wisdom becomes silence.
At this point, the Third Eye ceases to *see* and begins to *behold*.
The Crown opens, and the seer and the seen dissolve into one infinite awareness — the divine mirror through which God perceives God.

This was the true purpose of the Great Work: to transform human consciousness into divine vision — to awaken the immortal light within matter and recognize that Spirit was never apart from creation.

The Sacred Marriage: Ether and Light in Union

In the language of Western alchemy, the "Sacred Marriage" (*Hieros Gamos*) is the inner union of opposites: the Sun and Moon, Spirit and Soul, Consciousness and Form.
At the level of the Crown Chakra, this marriage is fulfilled.

- Ether corresponds to the Throat — the field of vibration, where thought becomes sound.
- Light corresponds to the Third Eye — the field of illumination, where sound becomes vision.
- Spirit corresponds to the Crown — the field of unity, where light becomes infinite stillness.

This union of Ether and Light gives birth to Spirit — not as a new creation, but as the remembrance of what has always been.
It is the moment when vibration ceases to move because everything has already been spoken, and light ceases to shine because everything has already been seen.
In that stillness, existence recognizes itself as divine.

This is the Crown's alchemy: the distillation of all experience into pure consciousness.
The mystic's voice falls silent, the vision fades into brilliance, and only the Presence remains — vast, luminous, eternal.

Psychological Alchemy: The Inner Path of Integration

Modern psychology reflects this same sacred ascent — a movement from expression to intuition, from self-awareness to transcendence.

- Heart Chakra (Anahata): Emotional maturity, empathy, relational depth.
- Throat Chakra (Vishuddha): Authentic expression, integrity between feeling and word.
- Third Eye Chakra (Ajna): Intuition, perception, and insight beyond intellect.
- Crown Chakra (Sahasrara): Unity consciousness — the dissolution of the separate self into universal being.

Each stage refines consciousness into higher coherence.
The Throat integrates emotion into communication.
The Third Eye transforms communication into awareness.
The Crown transfigures awareness into oneness.

Psychologically, this is the shift from *knowing about life* to *being life itself.*
The ego, once the narrator of experience, dissolves into the awareness that watches the story unfold.
This is the illumined mind, where wisdom no longer speaks in language but radiates as understanding.

The Crown therefore, represents the final stage of integration — when all opposites reconcile, and perception no longer oscillates between inner and outer, self and other, heaven and earth.
Only consciousness remains — whole, infinite, aware of itself.

The Universal Bridge: From Love to Illumination

Across mystical, alchemical, and psychological traditions, a single truth endures:

To perceive divine light, one must have spoken divine truth.
To speak divine truth, one must have first loved.

This ascending current — Heart $\rightarrow$ Throat $\rightarrow$ Third Eye $\rightarrow$ Crown — forms the ladder of illumination, the inner bridge by which vibration refines into radiance, and radiance returns to Spirit.

- The Heart opens you to love.
- The Throat gives love a voice.
- The Third Eye gives that voice vision.
- The Crown dissolves that vision into unity.

Together, they complete the Celestial Ascent of the Soul — the journey from compassion to communion, from resonance to revelation, from individuality to divine presence.

To walk this bridge is to participate in the Great Work of consciousness — the silent dialogue between heaven and humanity where all words end and only wisdom speaks.
Here, silence itself becomes the teacher.
Vision becomes prayer.
Light becomes love returning to its source.

Mystical Practice: The White Sun Meditation

(For the Crown Chakra – Spirit Realized as Light)

Purpose: To awaken the luminous stillness of Sahasrara and realize the unity of all perception.

1. Sit comfortably with the spine aligned, palms facing upward near the crown.
2. Visualize a radiant white-gold sun above your head — silent, vast, eternal.
3. With each inhale, draw its light down through the crown into the heart.
4. With each exhale, release the breath upward again as luminous vapor — your soul offering itself to Spirit.
5. Feel the exchange between Heart and Crown: love rising as light, light descending as peace.

6. Let the breath dissolve into stillness. Awareness expands beyond the body.
7. Whisper inwardly:

"I am the light beyond light.
I am the silence within sound.
I am the infinite perceiving itself."

Remain in that radiance until the distinction between inhaling and exhaling, self and source, no longer exists.

The Crown's Revelation

At the completion of the Great Work, the alchemist, the mystic, and the seeker all discover the same truth:
There is nothing left to transform, for all has been light from the beginning.

Sahasrara is the divine consummation — the "Philosopher's Stone" of the soul.
It is not attained through striving but revealed through surrender.
It is the moment the mind becomes translucent to Spirit, and Spirit smiles through every cell.

In that awareness, the eternal alchemy completes itself:

- Love becomes light.
- Light becomes stillness.
- Stillness becomes God.

"As above, so below;
as within, so without;
as the soul, so the light of Heaven."

To live through the Crown is to live as the Great Work fulfilled — the human soul crowned in gold, radiant with divine remembrance, the bridge between Heaven and Earth where all opposites are reconciled in one endless light.

Crystals for the Crown Chakra

LIGHT OF CONSCIOUSNESS – STONES OF UNITY, PEACE, AND DIVINE CONNECTION

Crystals attuned to the Crown Chakra (Sahasrara) vibrate with the highest frequencies of consciousness — the energy of spiritual illumination, divine union, and pure being.
They assist in merging the self with the Infinite, bridging the human and the divine.
These stones harmonize the subtle body with cosmic intelligence, dissolving separation and awakening the remembrance that consciousness is light itself.

Through their radiant frequencies, Crown crystals calm the mind, open the gateway to higher realms, and expand awareness into serenity, silence, and bliss.
They are companions of meditation, ascension, and enlightenment — the luminous allies that remind you:

"You are not the light you seek.
You are the light that is seeking."

CLEAR QUARTZ

Qualities: Amplification, clarity, divine awareness.
Known as the *Master Healer* and *Stone of Light*, Clear Quartz resonates with all chakras but finds its highest expression in the Crown.
It amplifies energy, clarifies thought, and aligns the entire aura with divine order.
In its presence, intention becomes illumination, and awareness expands beyond limitation.

Use:

- Place on the crown or hold during meditation to amplify clarity and connection to Source.
- Keep a crystal point on your altar to magnify prayer, Reiki, or lightwork.
- Pair with Amethyst or Selenite for deeper attunement to higher planes.

SELENITE

Qualities: Purity, angelic connection, divine light.
Named for the Moon, Selenite carries the serene radiance of celestial consciousness.
Its high frequency cleanses the aura, removes energetic stagnation, and establishes a pillar of light from Earth to Heaven.
Selenite opens Sahasrara to receive divine messages and integrates that light through the entire energy field.

Use:

- Sweep gently around your aura to purify and balance.
- Place above the head in meditation to channel higher guidance.
- Keep a wand or tower near your bedside to maintain spiritual clarity and peace during sleep.

AMETHYST (VIOLET QUARTZ)

Qualities: Spiritual wisdom, serenity, protection.
A bridge between the Third Eye and Crown, Amethyst stills the restless mind and guides awareness into divine communion.
It dissolves attachment and purifies thoughts, aligning the intellect with the soul's wisdom.
Its violet flame frequency transmutes lower energies into spiritual light.

Use:

- Place on the crown or heart during meditation to unify upper and lower energies.
- Wear as jewelry to maintain spiritual calm and energetic protection.
- Use in grids or Reiki sessions to raise vibrational frequency.

SUGILITE

Qualities: Divine love, spiritual protection, integration of higher consciousness.
Sugilite is often called *The Healer's Stone* because it grounds divine energy into physical reality.
It protects sensitive souls while deepening connection to spiritual truth.
Its violet-lavender hues radiate unconditional love and faith, reminding us that enlightenment and compassion are one.

Use:

- Hold during prayer or Reiki to strengthen divine connection and psychic protection.
- Keep near the pillow to aid dreamwork and soul healing.
- Carry when navigating intense energetic transitions or awakening experiences.

CHAROITE

Qualities: Transformation, service, spiritual strength.
Charoite embodies the synthesis of spiritual insight and earthly purpose.
Its swirling violet and lilac patterns symbolize the soul's evolution from chaos to harmony.
It assists in integrating high-frequency light into daily life, turning awakening into compassionate action.

Use:

- Hold over the crown or heart to align spiritual purpose with love in action.
- Carry as a talisman during healing or teaching work.
- Use in meditation when seeking clarity of life path or divine direction.

LEPIDOLITE

Qualities: Serenity, balance, spiritual attunement.
Containing natural lithium, Lepidolite soothes the emotional body and opens the upper chakras to peace.
It assists those experiencing spiritual overwhelm, transitions, or energetic sensitivity.
Its soft lavender shimmer reconnects awareness to divine rhythm — reminding you that all unfolds in perfect timing.

Use:

- Place on the crown or third eye during deep relaxation or Reiki attunement.
- Carry to calm nervous energy or overthinking.
- Keep by the bed to encourage peaceful sleep and higher guidance through dreams.

WHITE CALCITE / OPTICAL CALCITE (ICELAND SPAR)

Qualities: Purity, multidimensional clarity, expansion.
White Calcite refracts light into rainbows, teaching the soul how to perceive unity through diversity.
It enhances meditation, lifts depression, and clears energetic pathways for divine inspiration.
It is the crystalline prism of enlightenment — bending perception until all color returns to pure light.

Use:

- Meditate with Optical Calcite above the crown to magnify divine awareness.
- Hold in both hands when seeking spiritual direction or angelic communication.
- Use to harmonize a space before prayer or sacred ceremony.

Each of these stones embodies an aspect of divine illumination

Together they form a crystalline choir, singing the vibration of unity into every cell of your being.
They guide the consciousness beyond thought, beyond form — into the serenity of the Infinite.

"Through stillness, I remember.
Through light, I awaken.
Through unity, I am whole."

HOW TO WORK WITH CROWN CHAKRA CRYSTALS

Purpose:

Crown Chakra crystals elevate awareness from intellect to illumination, helping the soul attune to divine will and universal harmony.
Through them, meditation deepens, Reiki amplifies, and daily life becomes a living prayer.

Placement

Lay your chosen stones gently above the head or rest them on the pillow during meditation or energy work.
You may also arrange a triangle grid — one stone each at the Heart, Third Eye, and Crown — to align love, vision, and

divine consciousness.
During Reiki, hover a Selenite wand above the crown to
channel celestial energy and clear the auric field.

Light Charging

The Crown vibrates to the frequency of pure white or golden
light — the color of divine illumination.
Charge your crystals under the rising sun or beneath the full
moon to harmonize solar clarity and lunar serenity.
As they bathe in light, visualize a column of radiant brilliance
connecting Earth and Heaven through your own crown.

Whisper:

"Light within light, awaken in me.
I am the radiance of divine harmony."

Meditation & Sacred Space

Keep Crown Chakra crystals on your altar, meditation space, or
near your pillow.
They create an energetic temple — a field of purity, calm, and
expansion.
Use them during prayer, attunement, or silent contemplation to
deepen connection with higher planes of consciousness.

Visualization Charging

Hold your crystal above your head and imagine it glowing with
pure white light.
See that light flowing downward into your crown, cascading
through your entire being until you become transparent,
luminous, and still.
Breathe softly and affirm:

"Through this light, I transcend.
Through this peace, I remember."

Silent Meditation Charging

In stillness, Crown stones charge not through effort but through presence.
Sit with the crystal above your crown, allowing awareness to expand until both you and the stone are one field of consciousness.
There is no giver, no receiver — only radiance.

Affirm:

"In light, I dissolve.
In unity, I am."

Charging Affirmation

"Through divine light, I awaken.
My crystals reflect the wisdom of Source.
They amplify serenity, radiance, and love in all that I am."

Closing Reflection

Crystals of the Crown Chakra are mirrors of divinity — sacred fragments of cosmic intelligence crystallized in matter.
Through them, light remembers itself.
Their purpose is not to take you higher but to reveal that you were never separate from the light above.

"I am the crown of creation.
I am the stillness between breaths.
I am the light that knows itself."

Essential Oils for the Crown Chakra (Sahasrara)

The Crown Chakra responds to luminous, serene, and transcendent aromas that quiet the self and open awareness to the Infinite. These essences do not stimulate thought—they dissolve it—lifting perception beyond identity into still, spacious presence. Crown oils clarify, sanctify, and unify: they attune the subtle body to divine intelligence so that awareness rests as awareness.

They are fragrances of remembrance—scents that say:
"You are the light you seek."

CORE CROWN ESSENCES
Frankincense

Qualities: Illumination · Prayer · Devotional stillness
Frankincense clears psychic residue and gathers the mind into a single, quiet flame. It opens the crown while gently anchoring the body, making meditation steady and deep.
Use: Diffuse for contemplative practice; anoint the crown line (well-diluted) to invite silence and receptive grace.

Sandalwood (Indian or Australian)

Qualities: Inner peace · Non-attachment · Sacred presence
Soft, woody sweetness that slows the breath and turns awareness inward. It refines subtle perception without strain—perfect for long sits and mantra.
Use: Diffuse before meditation or chanting; apply (diluted) to the fontanelle point and heart to link love with transcendent awareness.

Myrrh

Qualities: Consecration · Stillness · Ancestral peace
Earths the high frequencies of Sahasrara so insights can
integrate. Depth, gravity, and holy quiet.
Use: Blend a drop with Frankincense for ritual; anoint
crown/back of neck (diluted) to seal practice in reverence.

Selenic/Lotus (White or Blue Lotus Absolute)

Qualities: Mystical union · Bliss · Subtle vision
A whisper of heaven—expansive, crystalline, and feather-light.
Lotus encourages effortless surrender into unity.
Use: Micro-dose in blends (absolutes are potent); anoint the
brow/crown before meditation or dream yoga.

Angelica Root

Qualities: Angelic protection · Guidance · Clarity from above
Creates a "chapel" around the aura—safe, clear, and bright.
Supports sensitive practitioners during deep work.
Use: One drop in a personal inhaler or diffuser for ceremonial
practice; excellent paired with Frankincense.

Spikenard

Qualities: Humility · Letting go · Night-peace
Biblical balm for the soul. Grounds the ascent, loosens
attachment, and invites holy rest.
Use: Bedtime anointing (diluted) at crown and soles; beautiful
in grief rites or after intense energy work.

Lavender (High-Altitude)

Qualities: Equanimity · Nervous system harmony · Gentle
opening
Bridges Third Eye calm with Crown clarity. Smooths the edges,

steadies breath, and invites lucid stillness.
Use: Diffuse at dusk; anoint temples/crown (diluted) to soften into meditation or sleep.

(Optional allies: Neroli for serene joy; Helichrysum for light-body integration; Palo Santo only if ethically sourced.)

HOW TO USE CROWN OILS

Diffusion (5–20 minutes):
Frankincense + Sandalwood for contemplative practice, or Lavender + Myrrh for evening stillness.

Anointing (always diluted 1–2%):
Touch the oil to crown, heart, and brow to align unity → love → vision. Sit in silence and let the breath grow subtle.

Inhalation Prayer:
Hold palms to face; inhale slowly. On the exhale, release identity into presence. Repeat until the mind rests as open sky.

Meditation Seal:
At the end of practice, place a hand over crown and whisper: *"I am That."* Wait three breaths before moving.

BLENDS FOR SAHASRARA

1) Pillar of Light *(devotion · daily meditation)*

- 2 drops Frankincense
- 1 drop Sandalwood
- 1 drop Myrrh
  Dilute to 1–2% in jojoba. Anoint crown/back of neck before sitting.
  Affirmation: *"Through stillness, I remember."*

2) White Lotus Breath *(surrender · blissful quiet)*

- 2 drops Sandalwood
- 1 micro-drop Lotus Absolute (toothpick swirl)
- 1 drop Lavender
  Diffuse very lightly or anoint crown (diluted).
  Affirmation: *"I open into the Infinite."*

3) Angelic Canopy *(protection · clarity in deep practice)*

- 2 drops Frankincense
- 1 drop Angelica Root
- 1 drop Helichrysum (optional)
  Use in a personal inhaler or diffuser.
  Affirmation: *"I dwell in holy light."*

4) Night of Peace *(sleep · integration)*

- 2 drops Lavender
- 1 drop Spikenard
- 1 drop Myrrh
  Diffuser or diluted anointing at crown/soles before bed.
  Affirmation: *"In rest, I dissolve."*

CHARGING YOUR OILS WITH LIGHT & SILENCE

Sunrise Blessing: hold the bottle at crown height; feel a white-gold ray filling it. Whisper OM three times, resting in the silence after sound.

Moon Bath: place the blend by a window during a waxing/full moon. Invite silver light to cool and expand awareness.

Candle Gaze: soft-focus on a single flame; when the breath and flame synchronize, let that glow flow into the blend.

Silent Consecration: hold at heart, then crown. No words—only presence. When the mind is clear, the oil is charged.

SAFETY NOTES

- Dilution: 1–2% for leave-on (6–12 drops per 1 oz / 30 mL carrier).
- Sensitivities: Angelica Root and citrus oils can be photosensitizing (avoid direct sun on applied areas).
- Medical: Myrrh may interact with some conditions; Sandalwood/Frankincense generally gentle. Patch-test; avoid mucous membranes; keep away from eyes.
- Pregnancy: Use minimally and consult a qualified professional.

ENERGETIC INSIGHT

Crown oils are not perfumes; they are prayers in liquid light. They do not add anything to you—they reveal what remains when everything falls silent. Used with intention, they turn the mind transparent and the heart luminous, so consciousness can know itself as peace.

Mantra to Pair with Aromatherapy
"Light within light, awaken in me.
I am the stillness that beholds all."

Crystal + Aroma Activation for Divine Illumination

(Crown Chakra – Sahasrara)

The Crown Chakra opens not through effort, but through *surrender*.
It awakens in the still point between breath and light — where

self dissolves into silence, and consciousness remembers its divine origin.

This ritual merges two sacred allies — crystals and essential oils — to purify the mind, elevate awareness, and align you with the infinite radiance of Spirit.

Preparation

Set aside 15–20 minutes in a peaceful, uncluttered space. Dim the lights or use soft white, gold, or violet illumination. Light a candle or allow gentle morning sunlight to filter through.

Gather the following:
• One Crown Crystal: Clear Quartz, Selenite, Amethyst, or Charoite
• Your Illumination Blend: Any Crown Chakra essential oil blend (e.g., Frankincense, Sandalwood, Myrrh, or Lotus in carrier oil)
• A singing bowl, bell, or mantra recording (optional)

Sit comfortably with your spine aligned and palms resting upward on your thighs.
Close your eyes and center your breath in the heart.

1. The Breath of Light

Inhale slowly through the nose, feeling air rise from the base of the spine to the crown.
Exhale gently through the mouth, releasing all tension and thought.
Repeat three times, letting each breath become softer, quieter, subtler.

Visualize a column of white-gold light descending through the top of your head — a luminous river of consciousness flowing

from Heaven to Earth.
Whisper:

"I breathe light.
I surrender into peace.
I awaken as pure awareness."

2. Anointing the Crown of Illumination

Warm a few drops of your Illumination Blend between your palms.
Cup your hands over your nose, inhaling the sacred aroma with presence.

With reverence, anoint these points:
• The Crown (top of head): Divine connection and unity.
• The Heart: Compassion, gratitude, and stillness.
• The Brow: Clarity and inner knowing.

As you touch each point, breathe light into it.
Feel the aroma lift your consciousness upward, dissolving all boundaries between self and Spirit.

Affirm softly:

"Light fills my being.
I am open, clear, and whole.
Through silence, I remember."

3. Crystal Resonance

Hold your chosen crystal in your left hand (receptive side).
Lift it gently above your crown or rest it at the top of your head.
Close your eyes and visualize brilliant white or violet light radiating through the stone.

With each inhale, draw that light into your body.
With each exhale, let it expand outward — through the crown,
through the aura, through the room — until everything glows as
one unified field.

Chant or whisper the mantra:

"AUM."

Let its vibration rise through your spine and resonate in your
crown, echoing into infinite stillness.
Feel yourself dissolving into luminous awareness.

4. Meditation of Divine Union

Place the crystal in your open palms, resting them lightly above
your head or in your lap.
Visualize a thousand-petaled lotus unfolding at the crown —
each petal shimmering with white-violet light.
From its center, light cascades downward, touching every
chakra, every cell, every breath.

Rest in the radiant stillness that follows.
There is no effort now — only being.
Only light.

Whisper:

"I am the light beyond light.
I am the silence within sound.
I am infinite awareness."

Remain here as long as you wish, allowing the boundary
between inner and outer to fade.

5. Integration

Bring one hand to your heart and the other to your crown.
Feel the current of energy connecting Heaven and Earth through you.
You are the bridge — Spirit in form, consciousness embodied.

Affirm gently:

"Light descends through me.
Love radiates from me.
Peace lives within me."

Take three grounding breaths, feeling gratitude rise from the heart like a quiet blessing.
Open your eyes softly, carrying this calm luminosity into your day.

Aftercare

• Cleanse your crystal in sunlight, moonlight, or sound (bell, mantra, or OM).
• Store your oil blend on an altar or near a Selenite or Quartz cluster to preserve its high vibration.
• Repeat this ritual weekly or after deep meditation, healing work, or spiritual study.

Closing Reflection

When practiced with presence and devotion, this ritual becomes a passage into the eternal — a remembrance that illumination is not attained; it is revealed.
Through crystal, aroma, and light, you rediscover the truth whispered through Sahasrara:

"You are not reaching for heaven.
Heaven is remembering itself through you."

Somatic Practices for the Crown Chakra

EMBODYING STILLNESS AND DIVINE CONNECTION

Where the Third Eye perceives light, the Crown Chakra
(Sahasrara) *becomes* it.
This is the realm beyond thought — the stillness from which
awareness arises.
Somatic practice at this level is not about movement, but
remembrance: allowing the body to dissolve into breath, and the
breath into being.

The body becomes a temple for consciousness; each motion,
each inhale, a silent act of devotion.
Through gentle, mindful embodiment, you awaken the felt
sense of unity — where energy flows without direction and
peace exists without reason.

The following practices invite surrender, spaciousness, and
presence — teaching you to feel light rather than seek it, and to
rest in the truth that you are already whole.

1. The Breath of Still Awareness

This breath unites heaven and earth through your body,
awakening the vertical current of light that flows through
Sahasrara.

Practice:

1. Sit or stand tall with your spine elongated, crown
    reaching softly toward the sky.
2. Inhale slowly through the nose, imagining breath rising
    from the base of the spine to the crown.
3. Pause briefly — feel suspended between earth and sky.

4. Exhale gently through the mouth, letting light descend through every cell.
5. With each cycle, awareness expands beyond the boundaries of the body.

Mantra:

"With each breath, I rise into stillness.
I am the space in which all life unfolds."

2. The Crown Touch: Remembering the Infinite

This tactile meditation opens the thousand-petaled lotus at the top of the head, aligning you with the subtle pulse of universal life.

Practice:

1. Warm your palms by rubbing them together.
2. Gently hover them a few inches above the crown — not touching, simply sensing.
3. Feel a soft tingling or magnetic pull; this is the current of Sahasrara awakening.
4. Inhale and imagine radiant white light flowing down through your hands into the crown.
5. Exhale, allowing the same light to cascade through the heart and into the earth.

Mantra:

"Light flows through me.
I am the bridge between heaven and earth."

3. The Descent of Grace: Body as Temple

The higher chakras are balanced not by rising *away* from the body, but by letting light *descend* into it. This somatic grounding integrates illumination with embodiment.

Practice:

1. Stand or sit with feet grounded and crown open.
2. On the inhale, imagine a column of light descending through the crown to your heart.
3. On the exhale, feel that light continue down to your feet and into the earth.
4. With each breath, sense the body as luminous — matter infused with spirit.
5. Rest in the gentle rhythm of breath as a prayer of embodiment.

Mantra:

"Light descends and fills me.
Heaven and Earth breathe as one within me."

4. Movement of Grace: Expanding the Field

This flowing gesture refines subtle energy, awakening the aura around the head and shoulders.

Practice:

1. Stand with feet shoulder-width apart, arms relaxed.
2. Inhale as you lift your arms wide and overhead, palms open to the sky.
3. Exhale as you lower your hands slowly down the sides of your body, palms facing inward, as if smoothing light around you.

4. Continue for 5–7 breaths, moving slowly, eyes half-closed, awareness resting at the crown.
5. Feel your energy expanding like a sphere of white-violet light.

Mantra:

"I am surrounded by light.
My presence is peace."

5. The Silent Heart Meditation

True integration of the Crown occurs when awareness rests in both heart and head — still, luminous, unified.

Practice:

1. Sit in meditation, spine tall, eyes gently closed.
2. Place one hand on the heart, the other lightly over the crown.
3. Inhale into both points simultaneously — heart glowing rose, crown glowing white.
4. Exhale and feel the two lights merge in your mind's eye.
5. Remain in silence for several minutes, listening not to breath or thought, but to *awareness itself.*

Mantra:

"I am silence.
I am love.
I am light."

ENERGETIC INSIGHT

In Sahasrara, somatic practice transcends movement — it becomes *presence embodied.*
When breath slows and mind quiets, awareness reveals its true nature: vast, radiant, whole.

The more you surrender, the more you awaken — not to do, but to *be*.
The body no longer seeks enlightenment; it recognizes it has been the vessel of light all along.

Through stillness, touch, and subtle motion, you remember:

"I am the consciousness that breathes all things.
I am the space between thoughts,
The silence behind sound,
The light within every breath."

Yoga Poses for the Crown Chakra

AWAKENING DIVINE CONNECTION, UNITY, AND STILLNESS

The Crown Chakra (Sahasrara) governs transcendence — the meeting point between body and spirit, self and Source.
Through gentle, meditative postures that open the spine, calm the nervous system, and balance the energy between heaven and earth, you awaken awareness beyond identity.
These poses refine subtle perception, encourage surrender, and align the entire chakra system — guiding you toward the pure consciousness that rests within stillness.

Each movement becomes a prayer of remembrance — an offering of body to light, of breath to eternity.

1. Easy Pose of Illumination (Sukhasana with Crown Awareness)

Sit cross-legged, spine tall, crown reaching upward as if drawn by invisible light.
Rest your hands on your knees, palms open to the sky.
Close your eyes and visualize a lotus of white or violet light blooming at the top of your head.
Breathe softly into this luminous space.
Each inhale expands light; each exhale dissolves boundaries.

Focus: Meditation, connection to Spirit, serenity.
Affirmation:

"I am open to divine light.
Stillness reveals who I am."

2. Mountain Pose (Tadasana) – Pillar of Light

Stand tall with feet grounded and arms by your sides.
Inhale and feel energy rising from your feet through your spine to the crown.
Exhale and imagine white-gold light pouring down from above into your heart and the earth below.
You are the bridge between heaven and earth — rooted and radiant.

Focus: Grounding higher consciousness, vertical alignment, unity of energies.
Affirmation:

"Light flows through me.
I stand as heaven on earth."

3. Tree Pose (Vrksasana) – Rooted in Heaven

From standing, shift weight onto one leg and place the other foot along the inner thigh or calf.
Bring palms together at the heart or extend arms overhead like branches.
Lift your crown toward the sky while grounding firmly through the foot.
Breathe deeply, embodying balance between earth and spirit.

Focus: Balance, grace, grounded enlightenment.
Affirmation:

"Rooted in stillness, I reach into light."

4. Supported Fish Pose (Matsyasana Variation) – Heart to Heaven

Lie on your back with a bolster or folded blanket beneath the upper back and head.
Allow your arms to open wide, palms facing upward.
Let your heart and crown expand toward the sky.
Breathe into spaciousness — surrendering thought into light.

Focus: Expansion, surrender, heart-crown alignment.
Affirmation:

"My heart opens, my mind dissolves.
I rest in divine peace."

5. Rabbit Pose (Sasangasana) – The Bow of Humility

From kneeling, round forward to place the crown of your head gently on the mat, hands reaching toward your heels.
Lift your hips slightly, feeling subtle pressure at the top of the head.
Let this posture humble the mind and awaken reverence for life.

Focus: Devotion, humility, awakening of the crown center.
Affirmation:

"I surrender my will to divine wisdom.
Through humility, I awaken grace."

6. Supported Headstand (Salamba Sirsasana) – Still Point of Awareness

If comfortable with inversions, practice near a wall for safety.
Place forearms on the ground, interlace fingers, and rest the
crown between your hands.
Lift into alignment, balancing through breath rather than effort.
Allow light to pool in the head — radiant, silent, serene.

Focus: Enlightenment, balance, calm concentration.
Affirmation:

"I rest in the stillness beyond thought.
I am light embodied."

7. Seated Forward Fold (Paschimottanasana) – The Descent of Grace

Sit tall with legs extended, inhale to lengthen the spine, exhale
to fold forward gently.
Let your forehead rest on your knees or a cushion.
Surrender tension and thought.
This posture teaches that true ascension begins with humility
and surrender.

Focus: Release, acceptance, integration of light through
surrender.
Affirmation:

"I bow to the divine within.
In letting go, I rise."

8. Legs-Up-the-Wall Pose (Viparita Karani) – Receiving the Infinite

Lie with your hips close to the wall and legs extended upward.
Rest arms by your sides, palms open.
Breathe softly and feel the subtle pulse of energy flowing
through the crown and heart.
As the body relaxes, consciousness expands.

Focus: Restoration, receptivity, alignment with cosmic flow.
Affirmation:

"I receive divine peace.
Light fills every part of my being."

9. Corpse Pose of Light (Savasana with Crown Awareness)

Lie flat on your back, eyes closed.
Allow the breath to slow until it becomes almost imperceptible.
Visualize a radiant field of white-violet light surrounding your
entire body.
Here, there is no doing — only being.

Focus: Transcendence, unity, integration of all chakras.
Affirmation:

"I am infinite awareness.
Light and life are one within me."

ENERGETIC INSIGHT

Crown Chakra Yoga is less about posture and more about
presence.
Each pose becomes a portal — from motion into stillness,
breath into spirit.
As the body opens and softens, awareness rises effortlessly,
connecting you with the Source beyond self.

When Sahasrara is awakened, yoga transforms from movement into meditation.
There is no separation between the one who breathes and the breath itself, between light and form, heaven and earth.

You no longer *reach* for the divine — you realize you were never apart from it.
Every pose becomes prayer; every breath, illumination.

"In stillness, I awaken.
In unity, I remember.
I am the eternal light within all things."

Healing Through Sound, Light & Lunar Cycles

HONORING THE ELEMENT OF DIVINE LIGHT AND THE RHYTHMS OF CONSCIOUSNESS

The Crown Chakra (Sahasrara) is ruled by the purest element — Light itself — the formless radiance that pervades all creation. Where the Third Eye reflects light as perception, the Crown becomes the source of illumination — the point where individual awareness merges with infinite consciousness.

This is the realm of transcendence, grace, and union with the Divine.
Here, healing does not come from doing, but from *being* — from surrendering into the luminous stillness that exists beyond thought, beyond time, beyond form.

Just as the sun shines without effort, your soul radiates without striving.
When Sahasrara dims, it is not from darkness but from disconnection — from forgetting your belonging to the eternal

field of light.
To awaken it is to remember that you are not separate from
Source, but an emanation of it — a living beam of
consciousness moving through form.

Through sacred sound, celestial light, and lunar reflection, this
ritual aligns your inner rhythm with the cosmic pulse —
restoring harmony between spirit and self, heaven and earth.

Light as the Essence of Healing

Light is the highest healer because it reveals there was never
anything to heal — only light forgotten.
It clarifies confusion, dissolves illusion, and reminds the soul of
its original wholeness.

Across ancient traditions, light has symbolized enlightenment
— the golden halo of the saints, the Sahasrara lotus of a
thousand petals, the crown of divine radiance.
Sound awakens vibration, but light awakens *consciousness
itself.*
Through Sahasrara, revelation becomes reality — awareness
becomes illumination.

In this highest teaching, light does not travel *to* you — it shines
through you.
Each moment of still awareness is not the search for God but
the remembrance that you are inseparable from the Divine
flame.

Intention for Practice

"I am one with Divine Light.
My being radiates peace, clarity, and unity."

LUNAR RITUAL FOR DIVINE ILLUMINATION
A Ceremony Of Light, Stillness, And Sacred Union

Perform this ritual during the full moon or new moon, when the veil between heaven and earth feels thinnest.
It harmonizes your inner rhythm with the cosmic breath — the eternal waxing and waning of creation.

You'll Need:

• One white or violet candle (symbol of divine illumination)
• A clear bowl of water (symbol of reflection and purity)
• A few drops of frankincense, myrrh, or lotus oil (to invoke serenity)
• One Crown Chakra crystal — Clear Quartz, Selenite, or Amethyst
• Optional: soft mantra, chime, or singing bowl tuned to 963 Hz — the "frequency of divine consciousness"

1. Prepare the Temple of Light

Create a peaceful space where moonlight or candlelight can softly fill the room.
Light your candle and place it beside the bowl of water.
Inhale deeply through the nose, exhale softly through the mouth.

Whisper:

"From the light of the universe, I awaken the light within.
From silence, I remember all that I am."

Add your chosen oils to the water or diffuser, letting the fragrance weave through the air like prayer.
Sense the atmosphere becoming sacred, clear, and still.

2. Awaken the Radiant Crown

Hold your crystal in your palms or gently place it atop your head.
Close your eyes and inhale through your crown, drawing pure white light downward through your body.
Exhale and feel it radiate outward, merging with the world around you.

Chant or hum the bija mantra "AUM" — letting it vibrate through the spine into infinite stillness.
Visualize a thousand-petaled lotus blooming at your crown, each petal a ray of divine consciousness opening to the cosmos.

Whisper:

"I am the light of creation.
I am peace beyond thought."

3. Communion with the Moonlight

Gaze softly at the reflection of the moon or candle flame upon the water.
See it shimmer — a mirror of your infinite self.
As you inhale, draw its light into your crown; as you exhale, release any lingering heaviness or separation.

Repeat silently:

"I release all that dims my radiance.
I am one with the eternal light."

Visualize your reflection dissolving into pure luminosity — no form, no thought, only awareness.

4. Descent of Grace

Lift your hands slowly from crown to heart, linking heaven and earth within you.
Inhale and imagine divine light descending through the crown into the heart's temple.
Exhale and feel that same light radiate through your aura, blessing all beings.

Whisper:

"Light descends through me,
Love expands from me."

Allow the body to rest in the quiet hum that remains — the soundless resonance of creation itself.

5. Seal in Stillness

Close your eyes, hands in prayer at the heart.
Listen beyond sound, beyond breath, beyond identity.
This is the silence of the soul — the eternal presence of Source.

Touch the surface of the water and say:

"From light I was born, to light I return.
I am whole, radiant, and free."

Pour the water back into the earth, giving thanks for the cycle of reflection and return.

Purpose

This ceremony teaches that awakening is not ascension away from the world — it is illumination *through* it.
The moon's light reminds us that we do not generate light; we *reflect* it.

In this reflection, we remember — light is not something to reach; it is what we are made of.

By aligning with lunar cycles, you honor both the fullness and emptiness of being — knowing that revelation waxes and wanes like breath.
To live in rhythm with light is to live as the expression of Divine consciousness in motion.

When Sahasrara is open, you do not seek enlightenment — you radiate it.
Every inhale becomes prayer, every exhale becomes peace.

Affirmations, Mudras & Daily Practices for the Crown Chakra

AWAKENING UNITY, ENLIGHTENMENT, AND GRACE

The Crown Chakra is the gateway to Divine consciousness — the infinite awareness that witnesses all experience.
When balanced, it brings serenity, connection, and bliss beyond reason.
When blocked, one feels disconnected, spiritually adrift, or heavy with thought.

Through sacred sound, gesture, and mindful devotion, the Crown opens like a thousand-petaled lotus — effortless, radiant, eternal.

AFFIRMATIONS FOR DIVINE CONNECTION

Speak these slowly with your palms open and crown lifted toward the sky.

Morning Illumination Affirmations
- "I am one with Divine Light."
- "Infinite wisdom flows through me."
- "I am guided by grace in every breath."
- "My spirit shines with peace and purpose."
- "I live in harmony with all creation."

Evening Surrender Affirmations
- "I release all thought and return to silence."
- "I rest in the heart of divine awareness."
- "All is unfolding in perfect order."
- "I am eternal, limitless, and free."
- "Light within me, light around me, light beyond me."

MANTRA FOR MEDITATION

AUM (OM) — *The Sound of Creation and Infinite Consciousness*

The universal mantra of the Crown Chakra vibrates at the frequency of divine unity — 963 Hz, the "God tone."
Chant softly, letting the vibration rise through the crown and dissolve into spacious awareness.

Focus:
Visualize a radiant field of violet-white light expanding above your head, connecting you to the cosmos.
Feel your body dissolve into this infinite glow — consciousness witnessing itself.

MUDRAS FOR BALANCING THE CROWN CHAKRA
1. Sahasrara Mudra — Gesture of Illumination

Brings balance to the nervous system and awakens the flow of divine light.

How to Practice:

1. Bring palms together in prayer and extend the index fingers upward.
2. Rest the thumbs lightly against the sternum.
3. Inhale light through the crown, exhale radiance through the heart.
4. Remain here for several breaths.

Affirmation:

"Light flows through me.
I am consciousness embodied."

2. Hakini Mudra — Gesture of Integration

Unites left and right hemispheres of the brain, balancing logic with intuitive knowing.

How to Practice:

1. Touch fingertips of both hands together lightly, creating a dome shape.
2. Bring the hands before the forehead or crown.
3. Inhale deeply, visualizing a sphere of white light expanding.
4. Exhale into stillness, merging awareness with peace.

Affirmation:

"All parts of me unite in harmony and light."

3. Padma Mudra — Lotus of Divine Heart

Symbol of purity and spiritual blossoming — connecting heart and crown.

How to Practice:

1. Bring the base of your palms together at the heart, keeping thumbs and little fingers touching.
2. Open the other fingers outward like a blooming lotus.
3. Inhale through the crown, exhale through the heart.

Affirmation:

"I am the lotus of light, open to divine grace."

DAILY BALANCING PRACTICES

1. Sunrise Stillness
   Each morning, face the rising sun.
   Inhale golden light through the crown; exhale gratitude into the world.
   Whisper:

"I live as light."

2. Evening Moon Meditation
   At dusk, sit quietly under moonlight or candle glow.
   Visualize your crown as a radiant halo merging with the sky.
   Repeat the mantra *AUM* until silence becomes your teacher.
3. White Light Visualization
   Imagine a river of white light flowing through your spine — from crown to root, from heaven to earth.
   Let it fill every cell with calm radiance and effortless joy.

ENERGETIC INSIGHT

Sahasrara teaches that awakening is not ascension beyond the human experience but the realization that Divinity *is* the human experience.
Light is not sought; it is remembered.
Sound is not heard; it is known.
The moon does not create light; it reveals what has always been shining.

When your Crown Chakra is open, you live as the embodiment of that remembrance — serene, radiant, and free.
You no longer reach for heaven; heaven breathes through you.

"I am not the seeker of light.
I am the light that seeks to shine."

Food Therapy for the Crown Chakra

NOURISHING SPIRITUAL CONNECTION, CLARITY, AND DIVINE LIGHT

The Crown Chakra (Sahasrara) governs the pineal gland, cerebral cortex, and the entire energetic system's communication with the higher consciousness.
It is the luminous gateway between the physical and the divine — the energy center through which cosmic intelligence flows into form.

To feed Sahasrara is to nourish the subtle body with purity, light, and intention.
This is not about eating more, but about *refining vibration* — choosing foods that uplift, purify, and quiet the mind so the soul may speak.

When balanced, you feel serene, inspired, and connected to the Divine — guided by intuition rather than appetite.
When imbalanced, one may experience disconnection, fatigue, brain fog, or spiritual confusion.
The goal of Sahasrara food therapy is to lighten and elevate, encouraging spiritual clarity, stillness, and unity between body and spirit.

At this level, eating becomes prayer.
Each bite, a conversation with light; each meal, an act of devotion.

Energetic Principles

- Element: Pure Light (beyond form)
- Sense: Universal Consciousness
- Color: Violet, White, or Gold
- Location: Crown of the head, extending upward into the auric field
- Themes: Illumination, unity, transcendence, bliss, divine connection

FOODS THAT HEAL AND BALANCE THE CROWN CHAKRA
Light-Infused Foods — The Frequency Of Purity

Sahasrara vibrates with light itself — nourished by foods that are fresh, living, and minimally processed.
These high-vibration foods carry prana (life force), allowing the body to feel lighter and the mind more serene.

Examples:
• Fresh fruits: pears, lychee, dragon fruit, and white grapes
• Light vegetables: cauliflower, mushrooms, fennel, and sprouts
• Coconut flesh and water for purity and hydration
• Natural floral infusions: rose, jasmine, or lotus

How to Use:
Eat mindfully, in silence or prayer.
As you taste, imagine each cell absorbing radiant light.
Whisper:

"May this nourishment awaken divine clarity within me."

Sattvic Foods — The Diet Of Enlightenment

In yogic tradition, the Crown Chakra aligns with sattva — the state of purity, harmony, and spiritual awareness.
Sattvic foods bring peace to the mind and brightness to the spirit.

Examples:
• Steamed vegetables, lightly cooked or raw
• Fresh fruits in moderation
• Whole grains: basmati rice, quinoa, millet
• Ghee and coconut oil (in small amounts) to stabilize the nervous system
• Almonds, sesame seeds, and pistachios (soaked overnight for digestibility)

Ritual Practice:
Before eating, pause and bless your food with both hands.
Visualize a beam of white light descending through your crown and infusing your meal with grace.
Eat slowly, without distraction, as an offering to the Divine within.

Purifying And Detoxifying Foods — Clearing The Channel Of Light

Sahasrara's physical correspondence — the pineal gland — is extremely sensitive to toxins, heavy metals, and overstimulation.

To keep this channel clear, minimize processed foods, artificial additives, and excess stimulants.

Examples:
• Warm lemon water in the morning for daily purification
• Herbal teas: lotus, lavender, holy basil (tulsi), and white tea
• Chlorophyll or wheatgrass juice for deep cleansing
• Fresh greens — spinach, kale, and parsley — to oxygenate and alkalize

Tip:
Drink your water consciously.
With every sip, visualize light descending through your crown, washing away density and restoring radiance.

Fasting And Liquid Light — Nourishment Beyond Matter

Because Sahasrara is linked to transcendence, periodic fasting or liquid nourishment helps lighten the body and heighten perception.
This is not deprivation but purification — a return to simplicity where Spirit feeds you directly.

Examples:
• Fresh-pressed juices with white or golden fruits and vegetables
• Herbal elixirs made with honey, lemon, and spring water
• Coconut water or rose water during meditation days
• Occasional mono-meals (one pure food, such as fruit or kitchari)

Practice:
Fasting during new or full moons deepens receptivity to light.
As you abstain from heavy foods, repeat softly:

"I am nourished by divine energy. My body is filled with light."

Spices And Herbs For Divine Awareness

At this level, subtle herbs elevate consciousness rather than stimulate it.
Their role is to awaken calm clarity, not heat or drive.

Examples:
• Saffron – raises vibration and brings joy
• Cardamom – calms the mind and refines prana
• Frankincense – spiritually cleansing when infused as tea or aroma
• Gotu Kola – known as the "herb of enlightenment," enhancing meditation
• Holy Basil (Tulsi) – purifies the aura and strengthens devotion

How to Use:
Infuse in teas, blend into light soups, or use aromatically before meditation.
Their fragrance acts as an invitation to divine stillness.

Foods Of Gratitude — The Practice Of Sacred Eating

True nourishment begins with awareness.
When you bless your food, you infuse it with your consciousness.
When you eat in gratitude, digestion becomes effortless, and energy rises naturally.

Practice:
Before each meal, close your eyes, inhale deeply, and say:

"May this food return me to light.
May every cell awaken to peace."

Eat only until you feel subtly full — never heavy — leaving space for prana to circulate.

ENERGETIC INSIGHT

Feeding Sahasrara is not about consumption — it is about *communion.*
At this level, food is no longer merely sustenance; it becomes a sacrament.
Every color, scent, and flavor is a frequency of Divine energy entering form.

When your diet is pure, gentle, and intentional, the mind quiets, and awareness expands.
You begin to experience food as prayer — the merging of matter and light.

As you nourish your body with clarity, the Divine nourishes your soul with wisdom.

"Eat light.
Breathe grace.
Remember — you are already nourished by the infinite."

This is the essence of Sahasrara — where food becomes radiance, and radiance becomes remembrance of your eternal Source.

WATER-INFUSED FRUITS AND LIGHT-INFUSED VEGETABLES
Cooling The Mind, Nourishing The Spirit, And Awakening Divine Clarity

The Crown Chakra (Sahasrara) is nourished not by heaviness, but by *lightness* — the luminous essence that purifies the body and uplifts the soul.
Hydrating fruits and gentle, high-vibration vegetables carry the frequencies of purity and peace, calming the nervous system while expanding consciousness.
They cleanse the physical channels through which spiritual

energy flows, cooling the mind and harmonizing the inner radiance of the subtle body.

To eat for Sahasrara is to partake in the communion of heaven and earth — where each sip, each bite, becomes a prayer of illumination.

Examples

• White grapes, pears, and lychees — foods of clarity, purity, and grace
• Coconut water, watermelon, and aloe vera — cooling elixirs that soothe the mind and spirit
• Cauliflower, fennel, lotus root, and asparagus — grounding divine awareness into the body
• Sprouted seeds, microgreens, and fresh herbs — symbols of renewal and ascension

How to Use:
Enjoy fruits raw or lightly chilled to preserve their prana.
Steam vegetables gently or eat them fresh, blessing each meal with gratitude.
Infuse pure water with slices of pear, cucumber, or mint and place it in sunlight or moonlight to absorb natural light frequencies.

As you drink, pause and whisper:

"May this water remind me of my source.
May this nourishment awaken the light within."

Each sip becomes a reflection — a sacred moment of remembrance.

Foods To Balance Excess Crown Energy

When the Crown Chakra is overstimulated, you may feel detached, dizzy, ungrounded, or overly absorbed in spiritual contemplation.
To restore harmony, anchor the light in the body through grounding and nurturing foods that harmonize heaven with earth.

Grounding And Restorative Choices

• Root vegetables such as carrots, parsnips, and sweet potatoes — connecting the celestial to the soil
• Warm soups made with lentils, barley, or root greens
• Herbal teas of chamomile, tulsi, or licorice — gentle bridges between thought and embodiment
• Cooked grains such as brown rice, millet, or quinoa — stabilizing the nervous system and grounding higher awareness

Avoid: Excess fasting, raw-only diets, or stimulants that detach awareness from the body.
True clarity arises from balance — not from denial, but from presence.

Ritual Of Sacred Drinking

Sahasrara resonates with reverence and stillness.
Transform each sip of water, tea, or herbal infusion into a ritual of remembrance — an offering to the Divine within.

Practice:

1. Hold your cup or glass just above your crown or at heart level.
   Imagine the water glowing with golden-white light.
2. Inhale deeply through the nose, exhale softly through the mouth, releasing all tension.
3. Whisper:

"Light within water, water within light.
As I drink, I remember."

4. Drink slowly, sensing the flow of cool radiance down the spine, harmonizing every cell with serenity.
5. Rest in silence, letting the afterglow of purity fill your mind.

Affirmation:

"Each sip awakens presence.
Each breath unites heaven and earth.
I am nourished by the light of creation."

ENERGETIC INSIGHT

Eating for Sahasrara is not an act of feeding but of *remembering.*
You are not sustaining life — you are celebrating it.
Water becomes light; food becomes prayer; nourishment becomes grace.

When you eat with mindfulness and gratitude, your meals transcend matter — becoming vehicles of consciousness itself. As you hydrate the body and calm the mind, you open the temple of the soul — where every taste, scent, and breath becomes divine communion.

Eat lightly.
Drink in peace.
Radiate light.

This is the nourishment of Sahasrara — where food becomes illumination and the body becomes a vessel of divine presence.

Herbal Bath for Illumination and Divine Connection

A RITUAL BATH TO AWAKEN LIGHT, SERENITY, AND SPIRITUAL UNION

This sacred bath is a ritual of purification — washing away the veils of tension and opening the gateway of the Crown Chakra. The water becomes a mirror of heaven; the steam, a bridge between form and spirit.
Through warmth, fragrance, and stillness, you are invited to dissolve into the quiet brilliance that is your true nature.

Ingredients:

• 1 cup Epsom or Himalayan salt — to release energetic heaviness and return to peace
• 1 tbsp dried rose petals or jasmine — to awaken divine love and devotion
• 1 tbsp dried lavender or chamomile — to quiet thought and soothe the mind
• 1 tsp lotus flower or white tea — to elevate vibration and connect with divine consciousness
• 3 drops frankincense or lotus essential oil — to enhance spiritual clarity and meditation

Instructions:

1. Add the salts, herbs, and oils to warm bathwater, swirling clockwise with your hand.
   As you do, whisper:

   "Light within, light around, light through me now."

2. Step into the bath with reverence.
   Feel the warmth encircle your crown like a halo of calm.

3. Close your eyes and breathe slowly, visualizing a radiant lotus of white-violet light opening at your crown.
4. With each exhale, release worry, fatigue, and separation. With each inhale, draw in serenity, surrender, and divine presence.
5. Rest in stillness. Feel the boundary between your body and the water dissolve into light.

Intention:

"May these waters cleanse illusion and reveal truth.
May I remember I am the light I seek."

When complete, let the water drain slowly.
As it flows away, imagine it carrying all that no longer serves you — returning it to the earth to be transmuted into peace.

Affirmation for Illumination and Healing:

"My being is radiant with divine light.
My mind is still and clear.
Each breath returns me to Source.
I am the light within all things."

This Crown Chakra ritual transforms the simple act of bathing into communion with the Divine.
Each droplet becomes prayer; each breath, illumination.
In this surrender, you realize — the water was never separate from you, and you were never separate from the Light.

Nature Practices for the Crown Chakra

Where the Third Eye perceives light through awareness, the
Crown Chakra (Sahasrara) *becomes* the light — radiant,
formless, infinite.
Its element is pure consciousness, expressed through the
luminous presence that pervades all of nature.
To heal and balance Sahasrara is not to *seek* connection, but to
remember that you have never been separate from the Source
that breathes through every leaf, ray, and ripple.

Nature mirrors this sacred unity — the quiet stillness of dawn,
the brilliance of sunlight through clouds, the hum of wind
across water, the endless horizon that invites surrender.
Each of the following practices guides you home to that
remembrance — not by effort, but through awareness.
Through nature, Spirit speaks — and through stillness, you
hear.

1. Sunrise Meditation: Communion With the Infinite Light

The rising sun is the daily resurrection of consciousness — an
eternal reminder that light never dies, it only returns.
Greeting the dawn awakens gratitude and divine clarity.

Practice:
• Sit or stand facing the sunrise. Close your eyes and feel the
warmth touch your crown.
• Inhale through the top of your head, drawing in golden-white
light.
• Exhale gently through the heart, allowing that light to flow
through every cell.
• Sense the sun's brilliance blending with your inner radiance
until the two are one.

Whisper:

"As the sun rises above, the light awakens within.
I am the dawn made visible."

Insight:
The sun teaches that enlightenment is not something you chase
— it is something that rises naturally when you are still enough
to receive it.

2. Cloud Contemplation: Surrender to the Infinite Sky

The open sky is the mirror of the soul — vast, boundless, and
ever-changing yet unchanging.
Watching clouds drift reminds the mind of impermanence and
teaches surrender to the flow of being.

Practice:
• Lie or sit beneath the open sky, gaze softly upward.
• Watch the clouds form and dissolve without labeling them.
• Breathe with the rhythm of the sky — expanding with each
inhale, releasing with each exhale.
• Let your thoughts drift like clouds, leaving behind only still
presence.

Whisper:

"I am the sky observing the clouds of thought.
I am boundless awareness."

Insight:
The sky is the teacher of spaciousness — showing that clarity is
not created by control, but revealed through openness.

3. River Communion: Flowing With Divine Grace

Flowing water mirrors the eternal stream of consciousness —
ever-moving, ever-pure, returning always to its source.
Connecting with rivers or streams reawakens trust in life's
unfolding.

Practice:
• Sit beside a river or flowing stream.
• Listen to its rhythm and let your breath follow its pace.
• With each inhale, imagine drawing in fluid serenity; with each
exhale, release resistance.
• Place your hand in the water and feel its cool current carry
your intentions toward harmony.

Whisper:

"As the river flows, so too does my soul —
never lost, always returning home."

Insight:
Water teaches that surrender is not weakness — it is alignment
with grace.

4. Moonlit Reflection: The Radiance of Stillness

Where the sun symbolizes illumination, the moon embodies the
serenity of reflection.
Sitting under moonlight opens the Crown to peace, purity, and
divine receptivity.

Practice:
• Sit in silence beneath the moon, allowing its silver light to
bathe your crown.
• Inhale the moonlight through your head and down the spine;
exhale through the heart, releasing thought.

• Visualize a thousand-petaled lotus blooming at your crown, each petal a soft ray of white light reflecting the moon's glow.

Whisper:

"The light of heaven reflects through me.
I am the stillness that shines."

Insight:
The moon teaches that reflection is the art of remembrance — that what you see illuminated outside is the same light within.

5. Wind Meditation: The Breath of Spirit

The wind carries the unseen — it moves through all things, unseen yet deeply felt.
Listening to it opens your awareness to the subtle current of divine breath.

Practice:
• Sit or stand in the open air, feeling the wind move across your skin.
• Inhale as the breeze flows toward you, exhale as it moves away.
• Sense that it is not just air, but Spirit breathing through you.
• Let each breath merge your being with the eternal pulse of life.

Whisper:

"The wind moves through me as grace.
I am breathed by the Divine."

Insight:
The wind reveals that separation is illusion — the same air that animates the world animates you.

6. Mountain Contemplation: Stillness as Majesty

Mountains are the great teachers of stability and transcendence — grounded in earth yet reaching toward the heavens.
To meditate with them is to feel both infinite height and eternal peace.

Practice:
• Sit before a mountain or visualize one rising in your mind's eye.
• Inhale from its peak, drawing light through your crown.
• Exhale down its slopes, grounding awareness into the earth.
• Sense yourself as both — the still mountain and the boundless sky above it.

Whisper:

"Rooted in earth, open to heaven.
I am stillness in form."

Insight:
The mountain teaches that awakening is not escape — it is the merging of spirit and matter in quiet majesty.

Affirmation for Divine Connection:

"The light above me is the light within me.
The stillness around me is the stillness I am.
I rest in oneness with creation.
The wind, the water, the sky — all breathe with me.
I am the Crown of light, the soul of silence,
the witness and the wonder of the Divine made visible."

Chapter 9 – Advanced Practitioner Applications

Divine Coherence, Quantum Illumination, and the Alchemy of Consciousness

For the advanced practitioner, the Crown Chakra (Sahasrara) represents the field of divine union — the integration of all perception into pure awareness.
Where the Third Eye transforms awareness into light, the Crown transforms light into *consciousness.*
It is not the act of seeing, but of *being seen through* by the Infinite.

At this level, the practitioner no longer interprets energy — they *embody* it.
Healing arises not through intention or intervention, but through the transmission of coherence — the resonance of wholeness that reorganizes all vibration into unity.

To master Sahasrara is to dissolve the boundary between seer and seen.
You become the stillness through which all frequencies align — the luminous bridge between Source and manifestation.
This is the Yoga of Union, the art of transmutation through presence: not light *as vision*, but light *as consciousness itself.*

ENERGETIC DYNAMICS OF THE CROWN FIELD

The energy of Sahasrara radiates as concentric waves of golden-white light — infinite, self-aware, and multidirectional.
It does not spin as a localized vortex but expands as a luminous halo, connecting the individual auric field with the universal grid of intelligence.

Within a client's energy field, this may be experienced as:
• A soft effervescence or pulsing at the crown of the head.
• Expansion of light upward, often felt as spaciousness or timelessness.
• Subtle oscillations of violet, silver, or white light merging into transparency.
• A sense of "dissolving" or merging with something vast and serene.

When balanced, the energy feels infinite, luminous, and tranquil — awareness rests in effortless unity.
When blocked, there is disconnection, cynicism, or spiritual fatigue — the mind seeks proof of what the heart already knows.
When overactive, there may be overstimulation, spaciness, or detachment from embodiment — too much transcendence without grounding.

Mastery of the Crown lies in the capacity to hold presence without polarity: to exist as both form and formlessness, rooted and radiant, silent yet aware.

LIGHT TRANSMUTATION AND QUANTUM ILLUMINATION

At the Crown, consciousness itself becomes the alchemical agent.
While the Third Eye transmutes vibration through awareness, the Crown transmutes vibration through *being*.
No effort is required; coherence itself heals.

In Sahasrara, light is no longer directed — it *emanates*.
You do not send energy; you become the field through which energy reorders itself into harmony.

Every thought, sound, or movement within this awareness carries the signature of divine intelligence.
Transformation happens not through will, but through entrainment — lower frequencies dissolving into the resonance of unity.

PROCESS OF CONSCIOUS TRANSMUTATION

1. Presence: Enter the still field of pure awareness. The mind quiets, breath slows, and all doing ceases.
2. Expansion: Feel light radiating from the crown in all directions — above, below, within, and without.
3. Union: Perceive that the light you emanate is the same light surrounding all beings.
4. Transmutation: Rest as the frequency of wholeness. Distortion, when met by unity, dissolves without resistance.
5. Integration: Anchor this expanded state into the heart and root, allowing illumination to descend into form.

"The healer does not heal.
The light does not seek to fix.
In presence, all things remember their perfection."

ADVANCED APPLICATIONS IN PRACTICE
1. Quantum Entrainment Through Presence

The highest form of healing occurs when two fields of consciousness synchronize.
In deep neutrality, the practitioner holds a steady vibrational field, allowing the client's system to entrain to coherence.

Practice:
Sit in silence behind the client, hands hovering near the crown.
Focus not on the body, but on the space around it — the luminous field of intelligence.
Breathe light through the crown, letting awareness expand infinitely.
No visualization, no direction — only presence.
Observe how the client's energy reorganizes naturally.

"As I rest in unity, all energy aligns."

2. Photonic Awareness: The Crown as Infinite Lens

Photonic awareness is the recognition that consciousness emits measurable light — biophotons of information and intention.
When the mind becomes silent, these photons transmit coherence directly into the quantum field.

Practice:
• Inhale light through the crown, exhale through the heart.
• Imagine the space between breaths glowing with golden radiance.
• Sense light communicating intelligence beyond words — truth traveling at the speed of stillness.

"Each photon of awareness carries divine intelligence."

3. Harmonic Transmission: The Silent Benediction

The eyes transmit Ajna's light, but the Crown emanates it.
In advanced healing, you become a resonant beacon of grace.

Practice:
During session, soften awareness at the top of your head and
allow light to radiate without effort.
This emission requires no visualization; it is a state of surrender.
Clients may feel tingling, peace, or sudden emotional release —
all signs of energetic reorganization.

"In silence, light moves of its own accord."

4. The Field of Unity Meditation

The Crown perceives no separation between healer and healed.
This practice expands perception beyond individuality into
collective consciousness.

Steps:

1. Sit with awareness at your crown.
2. Sense yourself dissolving into an infinite field of radiant
   light.
3. Whisper inwardly:
   "I am the breath of all things."
4. As awareness expands, feel every living being glowing
   within you.
5. Rest here — not as observer, but as the consciousness
   that contains all.

5. Divine Light Encoding

Sahasrara communicates through *light codes* — spontaneous geometric or crystalline patterns that arise during deep attunement.
These are not visions to interpret, but frequencies to integrate.

Practice:
During healing or meditation, allow luminous geometry to form in your awareness.
Do not define or analyze — simply breathe it in until it dissolves into wholeness.
This is the language of Source speaking through your subtle mind.

"The symbols you see are the shapes of silence."

ENERGETIC ASSESSMENT: READING THE CROWN FIELD

Perceiving Consciousness Through Light and Stillness

When attuning to Sahasrara, you are not reading energy — you are reading *presence.*
You perceive the quality of light above and around the head, the rhythm of the client's breath, and the level of surrender within the field.

Common Energetic Presentations:
• Dimmed Radiance: Disconnection from Source, spiritual fatigue, or loss of inspiration.
• Fragmented Light: Over-intellectualization of spirituality; disunity between knowing and being.
• Over-Expanded Field: Excessive transcendence without embodiment; dizziness or lack of grounding.
• Golden Harmony: Balanced Crown energy — radiant stillness, effortless joy, and compassionate neutrality.

The advanced practitioner reads not what is seen, but what *is felt* in the spaces between thought.
True assessment is resonance — an exchange of stillness.

THE DESCENT OF LIGHT PROTOCOL
From Transcendence to Embodiment

To work within Sahasrara safely, energy must always flow downward — integrating illumination into the physical body.

Protocol:

1. Establish Ground: Anchor the root and heart before engaging the crown.
2. Open the Halo: Visualize a soft sphere of light expanding above the head.
3. Draw Down Illumination: Inhale golden-white light from the cosmos into the crown.
4. Descend Through the Centers: Exhale that light gently through each chakra — crown to root.
5. Seal in Silence: Rest awareness in the heart. Feel the whole system vibrating as one harmonic field.

"Illumination is not escape.
It is light descending into form."

POLARITY INTEGRATION: THE PATH OF DESCENT AND ASCENT

At Sahasrara, polarity resolves — but it must be embodied to remain balanced.
The advanced practitioner learns to move energy both upward (ascension) and downward (manifestation), creating a constant current of renewal.

Practice:
• On the inhale, draw energy from earth to crown.
• On the exhale, let light flow from crown to earth.
• Continue until you sense no division between above and
below.

"Heaven breathes through earth, and earth breathes through
heaven."

LUMINANCE PRACTICE: EMBODYING SOURCE FREQUENCY

This meditation refines the Crown current into crystalline
awareness — anchoring divine frequency within the body.

Steps:

1. Sit comfortably, spine aligned.
2. Inhale through the crown, sensing infinite light entering
   the skull.
3. Exhale through the entire body, releasing into formless
   presence.
4. Rest in the stillness that remains — awareness observing
   itself.
5. Whisper softly:
   "I am the light remembering itself."

As you sit, all boundaries dissolve — breath, body, and being
merge into one continuous field of consciousness.
This is illumination embodied.

ADVANCED INSIGHT: THE STATE OF LIVING LIGHT

To master Sahasrara is to realize that there is no practitioner — only Presence.
Healing becomes communion; perception becomes creation.
The hands move because awareness moves.
The gaze illuminates because the light is self-aware.

When the Crown vibrates in harmony:
• Separation dissolves into unity.
• Thought becomes knowing.
• Knowing becomes peace.
• Peace becomes light.

You become the temple of consciousness — a vessel so clear that Spirit flows through without resistance, a flame so steady that even shadow becomes radiant.

"You are not here to ascend — you are here to remember that you already shine."

Hands-On Protocols for the Crown Chakra & Stabilizing Clients

Working hands-on with the Crown Chakra (Sahasrara) asks for the most delicate posture of all: *reverent neutrality*.
This is the center of unity consciousness—where light ceases to be an object of vision and becomes Presence itself.
Here, the healer does not *direct* energy; the healer *abides* as living stillness so the client's field remembers its innate wholeness.

The mark of a balanced Crown is quiet radiance: a soft, open halo of violet-white light; a felt sense of spacious peace; a clear descent of grace through all the chakras. When Sahasrara stabilizes, seeking relaxes, identity softens, and awareness rests in the truth that nothing essential is missing.

Client Preparation and Energetic Containment

Crown work expands consciousness. Before approaching the halo, establish safety, gravity, and gentleness so transcendence can land in the body.

1) Ground the Body, Invite the Infinite

- Guide three slow breaths: inhale through the nose, exhale through softly parted lips.
- Say quietly: *"You are safe to open. You are safe to rest. You are safe to receive light."*
- Encourage a comfortable, stable posture (support knees/ankles; place a light bolster under shoulders if needed).

2) Anchor the Vertical Axis (Heart–Crown–Root)

- Place one hand lightly over the heart, the other over the navel or sacrum.
- Visualize a column of pearlescent white descending from crown through heart into root and Earth.
- This establishes downward integration so expansion does not become dissociation.

3) Consent, Pace, and Options

- Explain you will work above the head and around the fontanel/crown sutures (highly sensitive).
- Offer hover-only alternatives at any time.
- Set a shared cue to pause, ground, or return to the heart if the client feels spacey.

Principle: Crown work is not a push through a doorway—it is an invitation to remember the open sky that was always there.

HAND PLACEMENTS FOR THE CROWN CHAKRA

Sahasrara sits at the apex of the skull and extends upward as a halo. Touch here is minimal; presence does the work.

1) Halo Hover (Primary Crown Activation)

- Hands 3–8 inches above the crown, palms facing down, fingers soft and wide.
- Feel for a gentle effervescence, like cool champagne bubbles rising.
- Let your breath slow until the field quiets; allow violet-white radiance to emanate rather than be projected.

2) Crown & Occiput Bridge (Descent of Light)

- One hand above the crown, the other cupping the occiput (base of skull).
- Sense light entering at the crown and nesting into the brainstem; allow the nervous system to melt toward parasympathetic.
- Ideal for clients who ascend quickly but struggle to embody.

3) Crown & Heart Link (Devotion Stabilizes Revelation)

- One hand hovering above crown, the other resting lightly over the heart.
- Feel the upflow of love meeting the downflow of grace; let the rhythm find you.
- This prevents spiritual euphoria from becoming ungrounded spiritual bypass.

4) Ear Chalice (Quieting Mental Static)

- Cup the ears very lightly or hover near them, thumbs toward the mastoid.
- Invite the interior of the head to become hushed—as if listening to snow.
- Useful when clients report buzzing, racing thoughts, or over-illumined crown.

5) No-Touch Crown Canopy (For Highly Sensitive Fields)

- Hands form a soft canopy above and slightly around the head (no contact).
- Perceive a sphere expanding; do nothing—Being does the rest.

Energy Movement Sequence: *"Descent of Grace" Technique*

A sequence for opening Sahasrara gently while ensuring light integrates through all centers.

1. Enter Still Field
   - Synchronize breath. Feel the room become quiet *with* you.
   - Inwardly: *"I abide in Presence. Presence abides in me."*
2. Open the Halo
   - Halo Hover above the crown; sense a cool, weightless radiance.
   - Allow the field to expand until effort dissolves.
3. Invite Descent
   - Move to Crown & Occiput Bridge.
   - With each exhale, imagine a soft cascade of white-gold light *down* through crown → brainstem → heart → navel → root.
4. Weave Union
   - Shift to Crown & Heart Link; let the heart's warmth and crown's clarity braid.
   - Whisper inwardly: *"Light descends; love receives."*
5. Ground and Seal
   - Sweep hands slowly down the central channel to feet, pressing gently into soles/heels (or hover at ankles).
   - Trace a slow figure-eight over the crown once or twice.
   - Affirm softly: *"Illumination embodied. I am whole."*

Signs of Activation and Release

Clients may report or display:

- Coolness, tingling, or light pressure at the crown.
- Breath deepening; face softening; tears of unprovoked gratitude.
- Spaciousness, timelessness, or the sense of being larger than the room.
- A quiet, natural joy; effortless silence.

Practitioner note: Resist the urge to explain. Silence integrates faster than words.

Stabilization & Aftercare

Because Sahasrara expands awareness, always complete with downward integration.

- Touch or hover at knees, ankles, and soles; invite heaviness and warmth.
- Offer water; suggest slow movements, a simple snack, and minimal screens for a few hours.
- Practices: gentle breath, a short walk, journaling one sentence only: *"What remains when everything is quiet?"*

Evening anchor: *"Light rests in my body. My body rests in light."*

Troubleshooting & Clinical Notes

- Over-illumined / spacey: Move immediately to feet, hips, and heart. Encourage nasal breathing, longer exhales, eyes open, name five tangible objects.
- Head pressure: Shift to Ear Chalice, then Occiput support; invite descents of breath to pelvis.

- Emotional swell with no story: Place one hand at heart, one at navel. Let the wave move without narrative.
- History of dissociation / trauma: Keep sessions short, emphasize Root/Heart, minimize crown exposure, obtain consent at each micro-step.

Advanced Insight: *Presence Heals by Coherence*

At the Crown, healing is not transmission—it is recognition. When the practitioner abides as unhurried awareness, the client's field entrains to unity.
Nothing is forced. Nothing is denied. All reorganizes around the memory of wholeness.

When Sahasrara harmonizes:

- Seeking yields to being.
- Concepts relax into knowing.
- Light does not arrive—it reveals.

Energetic Ethics & Boundaries for Crown Work

GUARDING SOVEREIGNTY IN THE FIELD OF THE SACRED

Sahasrara evokes awe. Awe can distort into authority if unattended. Advanced practitioners protect the client's sovereignty by embodying humility and clarity.

PILLARS OF ETHICAL CROWN PRACTICE

1) Sovereignty First

- Never present intuitive impressions as decree.

- Language frame: *"What arises in the field for you?"* rather than *"I see that you…"*
- Always offer opt-out of crown touch; hover is often superior.

2) Non-Appropriation of the Sacred

- Do not claim causality for grace. Replace "I opened your crown" with *"Your system allowed deeper rest; grace moved."*

3) Transparent Consent

- Explain possible experiences: spaciousness, quiet euphoria, or fatigue.
- Invite the client to set the pace (short crown windows, frequent grounding).

4) Clear Boundaries in a Boundless Field

- Before session: visualize a luminous boundary (clear, permeable glass) around your field: *"Clarity in, content stays home."*
- After session: brush the aura, wash hands/forearms, and let natural light touch your own crown for 30–60 seconds.

5) Mind the Power Differential

- If the client defers meaning to you, redirect gently: *"Your body is the oracle. What does this quiet feel like from the inside?"*

6) Avoid Spiritual Bypass

- Crown harmony is embodied unity. Always pair with Root/Heart.

- Encourage grief, tenderness, and everyday humanity to coexist with light.

RECOGNIZING ENTANGLEMENT & REMEDY

Signs: mental haze post-session, inflated insight, compulsion to teach, subtle exhaustion at the crown.

Remedies:

- Stand barefoot; exhale down the legs; name three earth textures.
- Place one palm at navel, one at sacrum; breathe 1:2 (inhale 4, exhale 8).
- Affirm: *"What is not mine returns to its source in peace."*

Post-Session Integration for Clients

- Drink water slowly; eat something simple (roots, warm grains).
- Sit in natural light or gentle darkness for five minutes.
- Write one line only: *"The most spacious moment was..."*
- Avoid big decisions for 12–24 hours if newly expanded.

Night mantra: *"I sleep in the light that loves me."*

The Sacred Duty of the Crown Practitioner

To touch the Crown—by hand or presence—is to stand at the threshold of the Ineffable.
Your task is not to deliver heaven, but to guard the conditions in which heaven is remembered—quiet, honesty, humility, warmth.

"When one field rests in wholeness, many fields remember."

Crown Chakra — The Role of Sahasrara in Remote Healing

CHANNELING UNITY, PRESENCE, AND WHITE-GOLD COHERENCE ACROSS DISTANCE

If Ajna perceives, Sahasrara (the Crown) *is*.
Remote healing at the Crown is not energy *sent* but Being realized—the client and practitioner meeting in one field of awareness. Where Vishuddha carries tone and Ajna carries light, Sahasrara carries Presence: the silent, white-gold radiance in which separation relaxes and wholeness becomes self-evident.

In distance work, the Crown functions as the aperture of grace: the point where awareness opens beyond personhood and coherence descends through every layer of the field. Here, nothing is pushed. The practitioner abides as stillness; the client's system entrains to that stillness and reorganizes around it.

Presence Beyond Perception

Ajna recognizes pattern; Sahasrara dissolves the knower. When the Crown is balanced in remote work, the practitioner notices:

- A cool, spacious bloom above the head; soft effervescence or haloing.
- Breath that becomes unhurried without will.
- An absence of imagery—clarity without content.
- A gentle descent of peace felt simultaneously by both parties.

This is not imagination; it is non-local coherence. In the Crown current, you do not project understanding—you abide as understanding and let the field remember.

"At the Crown, healing is the recognition of what never left."

Establishing Unitive Connection at a Distance

Preparation (2–4 minutes):

1. Root & Heart First
   Sense red roots to Earth; soften green light in the heart.
   Intention: "May what opens, land."
2. Open the White-Gold Aperture
   Bring awareness 6–12 inches above the head.
   Feel a quiet white-violet dome—no visualization needed beyond noticing.
3. Consent & Orientation (spoken or inward)
   "We meet in clarity, in the pace that feels safe. I listen more than I do."
4. Enter Shared Presence
   Instead of "linking" from your head to theirs, allow both crowns to rest in one sky—a field of white-gold spaciousness. Let the heart confirm the contact (warmth, ease).

Sustain: Rest as awareness. If images arise, let them pass. The *field* is the method.

Keeping the Field Clear

Distortion in remote Crown work arises from identification (trying to know, fix, or predict).

- Imagine the Crown as clear glass: light passes; content does not stick.
- Inner cue: *"I host stillness; I do not hold stories."*
- If analysis starts, drop attention to the pelvis/feet for three breaths, then return.

Closing the aperture: Inhale through the crown, exhale through the soles; feel the halo soften into the body.

Balancing Silence and Subtle Guidance

Ajna alternates light and void; Sahasrara abides as void that shines. In session:

- Rest 60–90 seconds in complete silence, then briefly notice what has softened.
- If "too empty," invite one breath of white-gold descending to the heart/navel, then release again into quiet.

Finish in stillness. Silence integrates faster than language.

Ethics of the Infinite

The higher the center, the lighter the touch—verbally and energetically.

- Offer reflections as felt qualities ("There's more ease in the breath") rather than cosmologies.
- Never imply authority over another's revelation. Phrase as invitation: *"What does this ease reveal for you?"*
- After the session, let meaning belong to the client's life. You carry only presence, not their narratives.

TECHNIQUES — CROWN-LED REMOTE HEALING
1) White-Gold Presence Field

Aim: Whole-field coherence without imagery.

- Rest attention above the head until white-gold stillness is palpable.
- Let that stillness include the client. No beams, no sending.

- Inner whisper: *"Presence recognizes Presence."*

2) Descent of Grace (Distance)

Aim: Embodied integration of expansion.

- From the shared halo, sense a gentle down-current: crown → heart → navel → root → feet.
- One breath per center; pause at the heart.
- End with warmth in the soles.

3) Crown–Hara Circuit

Aim: Prevent spaciness; marry transcendence and form.

- Inhale awareness at the crown, exhale to lower dantian (two fingers below navel).
- 7–12 cycles, then rest. The field brightens and lands.

4) Silent Benediction

Aim: Stabilize after emotional release.

- Place awareness above both crowns; speak nothing inwardly.
- Let a single wordless quality permeate (mercy/peace /innocence).
- Two minutes of pure Being; then ground.

5) Luminous Rosary (Counted Presence)

Aim: Maintain focus without strain.

- Touch thumb to each finger as you breathe one quiet presence per count (8–12).
- With each count, feel white-gold soften through scalp, face, tongue, heart.

Practitioner Re-Centering (Post-Session)

1. Retract & Return: Sense any outward radiance dissolving into Source.
2. Seal: One palm crown, one palm heart; 3 slow breaths.
3. Ground: Stand, bend knees slightly, exhale down the legs; feel weight.
4. Simple food/water; natural light on face/crown for 30–60 seconds.
5. Check humility: If grand or depleted, place palm at navel and affirm:
   "Grace moves; I remain human."

Troubleshooting

- Spacey client: Switch to Root/feet focus; name three physical sensations; suggest warm tea/simple carbs.
- Head pressure: Invite breath down the back body; visualize aperture widening then softening (never forcing).
- Flood of insights: Park them in the heart with one sentence: *"Let meaning ripen."* Close in silence.

Closing Reflection

Remote Crown work reveals that connection is original and distance is learned. The most effective "technique" is harmlessness, humility, and here-ness. When you rest as unhurried presence, the field remembers itself as one, and the body reorganizes around that remembrance.

*"Do nothing, change nothing—recognize what is whole.
In that recognition, all things come home."*

Clearing Ancestral Fear and Karmic Imprints

RELEASING THE LEGACY OF SEPARATION TO RESTORE DIVINE TRUST AND ONENESS

Where Ajna refines perception, Sahasrara (the Crown Chakra) dissolves perception into *pure knowing.*
It is the realm where spirit meets silence — where the soul remembers itself as the eternal witness. Yet even here, ancestral fear and karmic residue may cast veils over divine remembrance, weaving subtle illusions of separation, unworthiness, or doubt in the sacred.

These inherited shadows whisper, *"I am alone," "God is distant,"* or *"I am not worthy of light."*
Such beliefs are not truth but echoes of human pain — the memory of ages when the sacred was feared, forbidden, or lost in external authority.

Sahasrara carries the ancestral memory of spiritual exile — lifetimes of mistrust between heaven and earth, between the seeker and the Source.
To clear this chakra is to dissolve those old veils and allow grace to flow unimpeded through the lineage of light that lives in you.

"You are the answered prayer of those who forgot how to pray."

Ancestral Echoes Within Sahasrara

The Fear of God, the Fear of Self

Many lineages hold unspoken vows of separation — collective agreements born from persecution, spiritual distortion, or

misuse of divine power.
Generations later, these appear as subtle energetic imprints at the Crown:

- "It's safer to seek guidance outside myself."
- "Divine connection belongs only to the chosen."
- "To touch the infinite is arrogance."
- "Union with the sacred means losing the self."
- "To remember heaven is to betray the world."

These programs once protected the psyche from persecution or disillusionment. Today, they obscure the natural flow of grace. When unhealed, they manifest as spiritual apathy, fear of surrender, chronic disconnection, or over-intellectualized faith. Clearing them restores the innate trust in unity — the peace that surpasses understanding.

"Where your ancestors built altars of fear, you now build sanctuaries of light."

Karmic Themes of the Crown Chakra

The Journey from Separation to Surrender

Across incarnations, the soul learns to reconcile power and surrender, knowledge and humility.
The karmic story of Sahasrara often includes:

- Misuse of spiritual authority — claiming divine truth without compassion.
- Religious persecution trauma — punishment for devotion or revelation.
- Fear of merging with the infinite — loss of personal identity.
- Rejection of faith after betrayal by dogma.
- Attachment to enlightenment as an achievement, not a remembrance.

These experiences refine reverence. Through them, the soul learns that union is not conquest but communion.
The purpose of Crown karma is not to ascend higher, but to dissolve the illusion that one was ever separate at all.

Signs of Ancestral and Karmic Imbalance in the Crown Chakra

When these veils linger in the luminous field, one may experience:

- A dull or heavy sensation at the crown; difficulty meditating.
- Feeling "cut off" from guidance or meaning.
- Oscillation between spiritual euphoria and emptiness.
- Intellectualized faith without inner peace.
- Fear of surrender, of death, or of "losing control."
- Over-devotion to external teachers or rigid systems of belief.

These are not failures — they are thresholds.
The nervous system is relearning how to rest in the infinite.

The Path of Liberation: Reclaiming the Light of Grace

Healing the Crown from ancestral fear and karmic distortion means returning home — to the remembrance that *God is not outside you, and you have never left.*

1) Invocation of Remembrance

Sit in silence. Place one hand on the heart, one above the crown. Whisper:
"Through me, all generations remember the Light.
Through me, the Great Return begins."
Feel white-gold light cascading downward — a river of mercy washing through your lineage.

2) Violet-White Flame of Surrender

Visualize a luminous flame of violet-white fire spinning gently above your head.
With each breath, allow it to consume inherited fear of God, guilt, or separation.
Exhale grey smoke; inhale radiance.
Whisper inwardly:
"Only love remains."

3) Lineage Illumination Meditation

Imagine your ancestors gathered behind you, some radiant, some shadowed.
Inhale divine light through your crown; exhale it backward through the generations.
See it touching every soul — dissolving shame, restoring faith, reuniting hearts.
Affirm:
"May all who came before me rest in the peace of unity."

4) Mantra of Grace

Chant softly or silently:
"Om Shri Shanti Brahmananda"
("Infinite Peace of Divine Bliss").
Let the vibration ripple through the crown like sunlight on water, soothing ancient grief.

5) Water Offering for the Ancestors

Fill a small bowl with clean water.
Hold it at your crown, then lower it to your heart.
Say:
"As I pour this, I release all fear between heaven and earth."
Pour it onto soil, symbolizing the return of sacred memory to creation itself.

Energetic Healing Practice

Crown–Root Bridge for Ancestral Release

Because ancestral memory is held through bloodlines and earth connection, clearing must descend as well as ascend.

1. Inhale white light through the crown, exhale it through the feet.
2. Inhale from the earth into the heart, exhale through the crown.
3. Continue until the two currents blend into one rhythmic pulse.

Sense your lineage grounded in love, your spirit anchored in peace.

Integration: Living as the Bridge of Heaven and Earth

When ancestral and karmic imprints are released from Sahasrara:

- The fear of surrender becomes trust in guidance.
- The illusion of separation becomes oneness.
- The need to prove becomes peace in presence.
- The lineage of exile becomes a lineage of awakening.

You stand where heaven breathes into matter, where silence becomes creation.

*"You are the crown of your ancestors' becoming —
the moment when prayer, memory, and light finally meet."*

Affirmation of Divine Unity

"I release the fear of being one with the Infinite.
I forgive the past for forgetting its Source.
Through me, grace flows unbroken through all generations.
I am the bridge of heaven and earth —
whole, holy, and free."

Releasing Thought Cords and Restoring Divine Clarity

RETURNING TO UNITY THROUGH PURE CONSCIOUSNESS AND RADIANT STILLNESS

The Crown Chakra (Sahasrara) transcends even the subtlest layers of perception.
Where Ajna *sees*, Sahasrara *knows*.
It is the halo of consciousness through which thought dissolves back into Source — the luminous silence beyond interpretation.
Yet even here, subtle cords of thought, belief, or mental allegiance can cloud the purity of divine knowing.

These are not emotional attachments or empathic bonds, but spiritual filaments of identification — threads that bind consciousness to external ideas, teachers, systems, or collective fields.
When the Crown becomes entangled in such cords, awareness splinters into fragmentation — devotion becomes dependency, and truth becomes filtered through hierarchy or fear.
Releasing these cords restores inner sovereignty with the Divine, allowing wisdom to flow unmediated and whole.

"You are not a receiver of wisdom — you are the wisdom remembering itself."

Understanding Crown Thought Cords

Subtle Attachments of Belief, Doctrine, and Collective Consciousness

At the highest level of mind, thought cords form not through emotion or conversation, but through spiritual belief and identity.
They can appear as golden or silvery threads above the head, linking your awareness to:

- A religion, philosophy, or spiritual lineage.
- A teacher, guru, or belief system once revered.
- Collective energies of enlightenment or ascension movements.
- Cultural or ancestral archetypes of worthiness, sin, or divine punishment.

These cords are not inherently negative — some serve as *initiatory bridges* through which spiritual memory flows.
But when left unexamined, they may become channels of dependency or fear — preventing direct communion with Source.

When consciousness depends upon another's truth, the crown remains veiled.
To release these cords is not rebellion — it is spiritual maturity, the flowering of faith into direct knowing.

Recognizing Signs of Thought Entanglement

When the Crown Chakra is entangled in inherited or external consciousness, you may experience:

- Head pressure, heaviness, or tingling at the crown.
- Inability to meditate without imagery or external focus.

- Confusion about spiritual truth — alternating between devotion and doubt.
- Feeling "ungrounded" after group meditations or teachings.
- Seeking constant validation from outer authority or cosmic signs.
- Inner exhaustion after spiritual study, despite inspiration.

These are invitations to step out of borrowed light and return to your own radiance.

"When you release what you once worshipped, you begin to experience what you truly are."

Energetic Anatomy of the Crown

From the Thousand-Petaled Lotus to the Field of Unity

In Sahasrara, all lower centers converge — each petal a refinement of energy ascending through the chakras.
When thought cords constrict this flow, the lotus closes partially, trapping awareness between knowing and believing.
Releasing these cords restores the full bloom of the thousand petals — an open conduit between the finite and the infinite.

In this clarity:

- The need to define God becomes awe-filled silence.
- The mind becomes transparent, thoughtless yet alive.
- You no longer *reach for* divinity — you *remember* divinity.
- Awareness radiates equally in all directions — without center, without edge.

This is not emptiness; it is fullness without form.

Practice: Releasing Thought Cords Through the Crown

(Performed in reverence and neutrality — without judgment or rejection.)

1. Enter the Field of Stillness

Sit with spine aligned, hands resting gently on your thighs.
Inhale deeply through the nose, exhale softly through the mouth.
Feel the space above your head expanding — a soft sphere of violet-white light descending around you.

2. Identify the Thought Thread

Bring awareness to any belief, teacher, or concept that once defined your path.
Notice if your energy subtly contracts or clings when you recall it.
This is not disloyalty — it is consciousness showing you where freedom is ready to unfold.

3. Invoke the Light of Truth

Visualize a beam of radiant gold-white light descending through the center of your crown.
Whisper:

"Only truth remains.
All borrowed thought returns to Source."

Feel cords of outdated ideas, vows, or spiritual allegiances gently lifting — unraveling into pure light.

4. Bless and Release

With compassion, send gratitude to each energy or teacher once connected.
Say silently:

"I release you with love.
Your purpose is fulfilled.
I walk forward as living wisdom."

As you exhale, watch the cords dissolve into brilliance — no cutting, no force, only transmutation.

5. Seal in Radiance

Visualize your Crown as a radiant lotus of violet and white petals, open and luminous.
From its center emanates a golden column connecting heaven and earth.
Affirm:

"I am clear, whole, and connected directly to the Divine."

Sit in silence — not to listen, but to *be* the silence that listens.

Integration: The Mind Reborn in Light

When thought cords dissolve, belief transforms into knowing. The duality of "seeker and sought" disappears, and consciousness rests in its natural state — spacious, awake, and luminous.

In this clarity:

- Guidance flows without effort or question.
- Stillness becomes the teacher; silence becomes scripture.
- Every thought arises as divine play, not identity.
- You trust not in doctrine, but in direct experience of being.

This is the flowering of Sahasrara — the merging of intellect and infinity.

"The final vision is not of light — it is light seeing itself."

Affirmation of Radiant Awareness

"I release all cords of belief and illusion.
I dissolve dependency in devotion.
My mind is clear, my knowing pure.
Through stillness, I remember the One who sees through all."

Cross-Referencing with TCM

From Perception to Pure Awareness: Sahasrara through the Lens of Chinese Medicine

While the Third Eye (Ajna) mirrors TCM's Wood dynamic (Liver–Gallbladder) of *vision and decision*, the Crown Chakra (Sahasrara) corresponds more directly to the Spirit (Shen) seated in the Heart, the Sea of Marrow (brain) governed by the Kidneys (Jing), and the vertical Governing Vessel (Du Mai) that culminates at the crown.

That said, the Liver–Gallbladder pair still meaningfully influences the crown: their Qi circulates around the head, clears the sensory orifices, and provides the flexible assertiveness that prevents "spiritual dissociation." Think of them as *supporting winds* that keep the crown's lamp steady.

PRIMARY TCM PARALLELS FOR THE CROWN
1) Governing Vessel (Du Mai) & Baihui (DU-20) — Axis of Illumination

- Role: Lifts clear yang to the head, stabilizes the nervous system, unifies the spine–brain–crown axis.
- Crown link: DU-20 ("Hundred Convergences") is the apex of the Du Mai; it's the anatomical bridge for Sahasrara's vertical descent of grace and ascent of awareness.
- Signs of harmony: Light, easeful presence, quiet alertness, whole-body coherence.
- When disturbed: Scattered mind, agitation, "floating" Qi, insomnia, crown pressure.

2) Heart & Pericardium (Shen) — The Light that Knows

- Role: The Heart houses Shen (consciousness); Pericardium protects and softens it.
- Crown link: When Shen is settled, crown cognition becomes clear, non-grasping, compassionate.
- Signs of harmony: Serene devotion, effortless insight, benevolent clarity.
- When disturbed: Over-zeal, spiritual bypass, dependency on outer authority for meaning.

3) Kidneys (Jing) — Fuel for the "Sea of Marrow"

- Role: Jing nourishes brain/spine; anchors the ascent of light in substance.
- Crown link: Strong Jing prevents the "thin flame" of mysticism—keeps awakening embodied.
- Signs of harmony: Stamina in practice, grounded inspiration, deep rest.
- When depleted: Spacey highs, crashy lows, crown headaches, burnout after retreats.

SUPPORTING AXIS: LIVER–GALLBLADDER FOR CROWN CLARITY

Even though Sahasrara is not a Wood center, Liver (flow, big picture) and Gallbladder (decisive courage) keep the crown's light steady, clear, and non-reactive.

- When Wood flows: You can *release* images (Ajna) and *rest* in knowing (Crown).
- When Wood stagnates or flares: Temporal headaches, eye strain, irritability → crown feels noisy or pressurized.

Helpful Points (self-acupressure / light touch)

- DU-20 Baihui (vertex): Gather the mind into stillness; "plug into sky."
- DU-24 Shenting (anterior hairline center): Calms over-thinking before meditation.
- GB-20 Fengchi (base of skull, bilateral): Clears head wind, relaxes sense gates.
- LV-3 Taichong (top of foot): Moves Liver Qi; drops reactivity.
- PC-6 Neiguan (inner forearm): Settles Shen, releases chest-head tension.
- KI-1 Yongquan (sole): Grounds crown light into body; great post-practice.
- KI-3 Taixi (ankle): Tonifies Kidney Jing for sustained clarity.

How: 30–60 seconds of gentle, steady pressure with slow nasal breathing; less is more.

PRACTICAL HARMONIZING PROTOCOLS
1) Crown–Root Circuit (Du–Kidney Integration)

- Touch DU-20 lightly; breathe up the spine on inhale.
- Exhale attention to KI-1 (soles).
- 9–12 breaths. *Result:* bright crown, heavy feet—clear yet grounded.

2) Calm Shen, Open Crown (Heart–Crown Bridge)

- Hand on Heart, other palm hovering over crown.
- Inhale: "I soften." Exhale: "I open."
- Feel warmth rise, light descend. *Result:* devotion without drift.

3) Clear the Head Gates (Wood Support for Crown)

- Massage GB-20 → temples → DU-24 in that order.
- Finish with a feather-light tap at DU-20.
- Sip chrysanthemum + mint or peppermint tea. *Result:* clean, quiet dome.

4) Microcosmic Stillness (Du Mai settle)

- Sit tall; tip of tongue to palate.
- Breathe as if the inhale gathers to the crown and the exhale spreads like dawn across scalp and skin.
- No visualization needed—just the *feeling* of spacious presence.

HERBAL & LIFESTYLE NOTES (TCM-INFORMED)

- To settle Shen: reishi (lingzhi), jujube seed (suan zao ren), lily bulb (bai he), lotus seed.
- To clear head wind/heat (support Wood): chrysanthemum (ju hua), mint (bo he), gardenia (for heat; consult practitioner).
- To nourish Jing: black sesame, walnuts, goji, bone broths (or mineral-rich veg broths), deep sleep before 11pm.
- Avoid: late-night screens, excess stimulants, debate spirals—these scatter Du-20 and agitate Wood.

RED FLAGS & REBALANCING

- Floating crown / "too open": Pair DU-20 with KI-1 or hold a warm pack on lower belly. Eat something warm and simple.
- Crown pressure + irritability: Work LV-3 and GB-20 first, then very brief contact at DU-20.
- After big openings: Walk barefoot on earth; slow exhale twice as long as inhale.

MANTRAS & AFFIRMATIONS

- Shen-Settling: *"My mind is a clear sky; awareness shines without effort."*
- Wood Support: *"I move like water and decide like light."*
- Crown Alignment: *"I am the silence that knows."*

One-Page Practice (Daily, 5–7 minutes)

1. GB-20 massage (30s each) → DU-24 (30s).
2. Heart–Crown breath (1 minute).
3. DU-20 ↔ KI-1 circuit (9 breaths).
4. Sit 2–3 minutes in simple awareness; finish by pressing LV-3 (20s each).

Effect: Liver–Gallbladder smooth the wind, Kidneys anchor the light, Heart clarifies the knowing, Du Mai crowns the whole— Sahasrara rests open, quiet, and luminously human.

Chapter 10 – Transformation Through Sahasrara

Transformation Through Sahasrara

Case Studies: Awakening Consciousness, Faith, and Divine Integration

The Crown Chakra (Sahasrara) represents transcendence — the realization that awareness is not something we reach, but what we already are.
Where Ajna refines perception into insight, Sahasrara dissolves perception into unity. It is the moment consciousness recognizes itself as light.

Transformation at this level is subtle yet profound. It's not the awakening of new abilities, but the *dissolution of illusion* — the quiet understanding that there was never separation between self and Source.
Through healing and activation of Sahasrara, clients often experience deep peace, restored faith, and spontaneous clarity that cannot be taught — only remembered.

The following case studies illustrate how balancing the Crown Chakra facilitates integration between spirit and form, and transforms seeking into being.

CASE STUDY 1 – FROM SPIRITUAL CONFUSION TO DIVINE CLARITY

Client Presentation:
A 38-year-old yoga instructor described feeling "spiritually lost" after years of seeking guidance from multiple traditions. She experienced frequent crown tingling, pressure, and episodes of exhaustion following meditation retreats. "I feel like I'm chasing enlightenment," she said, "but I'm getting more confused."

Assessment:
Energetic mapping revealed excessive upward flow — strong activity from Heart to Crown, but little grounding through Root or Sacral centers. Her energy resembled a flame without a base — brilliant but unstable.

Therapeutic Process:

- Grounding Crown Energy: Combined Reiki for the lower chakras with visualization of roots anchoring light into the Earth.
- Crown Recalibration: Soft Reiki placement at the crown with slow breath cycles, allowing the energy to descend through the spine (Du Mai channel).
- Silent Integration Meditation: Ten minutes of breath awareness following each session — observing without expectation.
- Faith Journaling: Daily reflection on the prompt, *"Where do I already feel connected to something greater?"*

Outcome:
Within four sessions, the client's symptoms eased. She reported, "I stopped chasing experiences — now I just feel them arise naturally." Fatigue subsided, and she felt grounded yet illuminated.

Transformation:
Seeking became surrender.
The mind no longer reached upward for proof; awareness rested in silent knowing.

CASE STUDY 2 – REBUILDING FAITH AFTER SPIRITUAL TRAUMA

Client Presentation:
A 52-year-old man came after leaving a controlling spiritual community. He felt betrayed by false leadership and had lost faith in all forms of spirituality. "Every time I hear words like 'divine' or 'light,' I feel anger."

Assessment:
Energetically, the Crown field appeared contracted — dim, opaque, and shielded. His Heart was guarded, and a subtle heaviness pressed downward at DU-20 (the crown point), reflecting disillusionment and grief.

Therapeutic Process:

- Heart–Crown Connection: Began with Heart-centered Reiki and forgiveness meditation before addressing the Crown.
- Restoring Trust in Light: Used violet-gold visualization, gently reintroducing the concept of personal divinity rather than external authority.
- Mantra Practice: Soft repetition of "Om Shanti Om" to soothe the nervous system and restore trust in vibration itself.
- Earthing Ritual: Ending sessions with barefoot walking and gratitude for simple life moments.

Outcome:
After two months, the client reported meditating peacefully for the first time in years. "I feel safe inside my own silence now,"

he said. Emotional outbursts ceased, and creativity (music writing) returned.

Transformation:
Anger became awe.
Through gentle reconnection, faith was no longer a concept — it became lived experience.

CASE STUDY 3 – FROM OVERTHINKING TO PURE PRESENCE

Client Presentation:
A 44-year-old author reported difficulty focusing on creative work, insomnia, and overactive mental loops about the future. Despite practicing meditation for years, she said, "My mind never shuts off — even during silence."

Assessment:
Energetic scan revealed overstimulation of the Third Eye and weak energy flow through the Crown. Ajna was functioning, but disconnected — insight without surrender.

Therapeutic Process:

- Crown Breathing Practice: Inhale light through the crown; exhale through the soles of the feet — balancing upward and downward currents.
- Stillness Attunement: Reiki over the crown with guidance to release each thought as a petal falling into infinite space.
- Mind–Light Meditation: Focus on the affirmation, "I am the space where thought appears."
- Hydration & Sleep Hygiene: Encouraged warm evening teas (lotus seed, reishi) and reduced blue light before bed to calm Shen.

Outcome:
Within three sessions, sleep normalized, and the client reported spontaneous bursts of inspiration. She described a "soft hum of peace behind every thought."

Transformation:
Overthinking became overglowing.
Thoughts still arose, but they no longer bound her — they floated like clouds in an infinite sky.

INSIGHT FOR PRACTITIONERS

The Crown Chakra invites both client and practitioner into humility before the mystery.
Healing here is never imposed — it unfolds naturally as readiness ripens.

The practitioner's role is not to *awaken* another, but to hold a field of coherence so the soul remembers its own light.
Techniques may guide, but only presence heals.

When Sahasrara opens in harmony with the lower chakras:

- The nervous system stabilizes.
- The heart expands without collapsing.
- Intuition integrates with reason.
- Faith replaces striving.

True transformation at the Crown is not transcendence *away* from life — it is illumination *through* it.
You become a vessel of peace — grounded in matter, radiant in spirit.

"When the crown opens, there is no teacher and student, no seeker and found.
There is only consciousness, looking at itself, and smiling."

Chapter 11 – Reflection & Integration

Crown Chakra – Reflection & Integration

Daily Self-Care Rituals for Divine Connection and Inner Illumination

Healing the Crown Chakra (Sahasrara) is not an endpoint — it is the continual unfolding of consciousness into unity.
Where the Third Eye perceives light, the Crown *becomes* light.
Sahasrara governs awareness, faith, and spiritual coherence — the living experience of oneness beyond thought.

Daily self-care for the Crown is about quiet devotion, surrender, and remembrance.
It is the gentle refinement of your inner atmosphere — clearing static, calming the mind, and allowing divine intelligence to flow through you.
These practices nurture luminous awareness, strengthen faith, and align you with the rhythm of higher consciousness.

1. Morning Descent Of Light

Begin your day as an instrument of divine flow.

- Awareness: Before rising, place one hand over your heart and one over your crown.
- Breath: Inhale through the crown — soft, radiant light entering the body.

Exhale through the heart — light expanding through love.

- Intention: Whisper,
  "May I live today as light in form.
  May peace guide my thoughts, and grace move through my actions."

This morning communion harmonizes upper and lower energy currents — spirit descending into matter, and matter awakening to spirit.

2. Crown Journaling Practice

Sahasrara thrives through reflection that transcends reason — sacred contemplation.
Each day, record quiet moments of connection and realization.

Prompts:

- What feels sacred in my life today?
- When did I experience peace for no reason?
- What truth revealed itself in stillness?
- How did grace guide my choices?

Do not analyze — simply witness.
Your words become prayer; your reflections, revelation.

3. Light Immersion Rituals

The Crown corresponds to pure light — clear, radiant, uncolored.
Invite this element into daily life to replenish divine connection.

- Dawn Stillness: Sit where morning light touches you. Feel it crown your head like a blessing.

- Violet or White Lotus Visualization: Imagine a thousand-petaled lotus blooming above your head, each petal shimmering with golden-violet hues.
- Sacred Oils or Mist: Anoint the crown lightly with lotus, frankincense, or myrrh to honor the spirit within.
- Candle Meditation: Focus on the flame, then close your eyes and visualize its glow radiating through the top of your head into infinite space.

Affirmation:
"I am light aware of itself.
Through stillness, I return to truth."

4. Breath Of Union (Crown–Root Balancing)

To sustain higher awareness, the light of Sahasrara must anchor into the earth.

- Sit upright, spine tall.
- Inhale: Draw light from the crown to the heart.
- Exhale: Send it downward through the spine to the root.
- Inhale again: Draw grounding energy upward from the root to the crown.
- Continue for 7 cycles, creating a loop of golden-white current.

This breath aligns heaven and earth within your body — balancing transcendence with embodiment.

Affirmation:
"Heaven moves through me.
Earth supports me.
I am the meeting point of both."

5. Midday Silence Practice

Pause in the midst of activity to reconnect to the ever-present stillness.

- Close your eyes and take three slow breaths.
- Visualize a halo of soft white light above your head.
- Rest awareness in that space — no words, no effort.
- Let silence breathe you.

Even two minutes of this practice recalibrates the nervous system, reawakening peace and presence.

Affirmation:
"In silence, I remember who I am."

6. Evening Gratitude And Release

As the day closes, open the crown gently to release residual thoughts.

- Sit quietly with palms facing upward.
- Inhale light through the crown, exhale it through the soles of the feet.
- Whisper softly,
  *"All experiences return to light.
  I rest in divine peace."*
- Offer gratitude for every lesson, knowing each moment was guided by a higher rhythm.

Affirmation:
*"I release the day into divine order.
My spirit rests in infinite peace."*

7. Weekly Spirit Renewal

Once a week, dedicate time to the sacred — a ritual of reconnection to the infinite.

Practices:

- Meditate in Candlelight: Focus on a single flame until thoughts dissolve.
- Water Blessing: Pour water over your hands, imagining it washing away old energies.
- Nature Communion: Sit beneath open sky, feeling light stream through your crown into earth.
- Silent Prayer: Speak nothing — simply allow love to radiate outward in stillness.

Affirmation:
"I am whole, holy, and connected to all life."

Integration Insight

Sahasrara's awakening is not escape — it is embodiment of grace.
When this chakra is balanced, the ordinary becomes sacred: each breath, each glance, each word a reflection of the One.
Daily care at this level cultivates awareness that is luminous, humble, and free.

When you live from the Crown:

- Thoughts dissolve into peace.
- Intuition merges with faith.
- Every action arises from stillness.
- You no longer seek the divine — you *remember* you are it.

"When my mind rests in silence, I hear the voice of eternity. When my heart opens to light, I live as the light itself."

Journaling Prompts for the Crown Chakra

AWAKENING UNITY, FAITH, AND HIGHER CONSCIOUSNESS

1. Divine Connection
   - When do I feel most connected to something greater than myself?
   - What helps me experience trust in life's unfolding?
   - How do I recognize divine guidance in daily events?
2. Faith and Surrender
   - Where in my life am I still trying to control what must be released?
   - What does true surrender mean to me?
   - How do I balance faith with personal responsibility?
3. Silence and Knowing
   - What arises when I sit in silence without seeking results?
   - How does my mind react to stillness?
   - What truths become clear when thought subsides?
4. Unity and Compassion
   - How can I perceive others through the lens of unity rather than difference?
   - What judgments can I release to experience greater peace?
   - How does compassion expand my awareness?
5. Integration of Light and Life
   - How can I bring spiritual awareness into ordinary tasks?

- o What simple actions remind me that the sacred is everywhere?
- o What does living as light mean for me personally?
6. Reflections on Grace
    - o What recent challenge revealed hidden wisdom?
    - o How have I been supported by unseen forces?
    - o Where can I offer gratitude today?
7. Affirmations for the Crown
    - o "I am one with all that is."
    - o "Light flows through me, for I am light."
    - o "I trust divine timing and infinite intelligence."
    - o "Stillness reveals the truth that never changes."
    - o "Through faith and awareness, I embody peace."

Integration Note

Reflection at the level of Sahasrara is the art of remembering — not learning.
You are not trying to reach enlightenment; you are rediscovering it in every breath.

Let your daily rituals become moments of communion with the infinite.
Let journaling become sacred conversation.
Let silence become your teacher.

"When I rest in awareness, I remember eternity.
When I live in gratitude, I become light made human."

Chapter 12 – Understanding the Journey So Far

How Awareness Rises from Expression to Illumination

You've walked the spiral of Involution—love descending into form—and begun the ascent of Evolution—form returning to light.

At Vishuddha (Throat), love found its voice.

As energy rose into Ajna (Third Eye), voice became vision, and truth turned to insight.

Now, through Sahasrara (Crown), vision becomes illumination and awareness returns to its Source.

Communication has turned inward: from speaking to perceiving, from resonance to realization, from perception to pure being.

Where the Throat teaches expression through sound, and the Third Eye perception through light, the Crown reveals unity through consciousness itself.

FROM SOUND TO SIGHT TO SILENCE: THE SHIFT FROM ETHER TO LIGHT TO CONSCIOUSNESS

- Throat (Ether): We speak truth; vibration becomes resonance.
- Third Eye (Light): We see truth; resonance refines into illumination.
- Crown (Consciousness): We become truth; illumination dissolves into unity.

At Sahasrara, energy no longer seeks to express or perceive — it simply *is*.
Fire transformed matter.
Ether refined vibration.
Light revealed meaning.
Consciousness unites them all.

Here, the lens of the Third Eye dissolves into the boundless sky of awareness — the field where seer, seeing, and seen are one.

THE SEVENFOLD JOURNEY (A LIVING BRIDGE OF LOVE)

Book	Chakra	Element	Primary Lesson	Evolutionary Integration at the Crown
1. Heart Chakra 101 – *The Bridge*	Heart	Air	Love & Compassion	Love expands into universal empathy
2. Root Chakra 101 –	Root	Earth	Grounding & Belonging	Stability becomes

Book	Chakra	Element	Primary Lesson	Evolutionary Integration at the Crown
Foundation				trust in divine order
3. Sacral Chakra 101 – *Flow*	Sacral	Water	Emotion & Creativity	Feeling becomes devotion
4. Solar Plexus Chakra 101 – *Power*	Solar Plexus	Fire	Will & Transformation	Will becomes surrender to higher purpose
5. Throat Chakra 101 – *Truth*	Throat	Ether	Expression & Purification	Sound becomes silence — truth realized
6. Third Eye Chakra 101 – *Vision*	Third Eye	Light	Perception & Wisdom	Insight merges into still awareness
7. Crown Chakra 101 – *Unity*	Crown	Consciousness	Oneness & Faith	Awareness returns to Source — all is One

Each level has been a note in the symphony of awakening, each refining love through a different octave of experience — from Earth to Heaven, from form to formlessness.

The Three Great Triads – The Architecture of Awakening

THE JOURNEY OF ENERGY FROM FORM TO LIGHT, FROM LOVE TO UNITY

The seven chakras are not isolated centers of power, but a single current of consciousness unfolding through three sacred triads — each with its own purpose, rhythm, and revelation. Together, they form the vertical axis of human evolution, where Spirit experiences itself through form, and form remembers itself as Spirit.

Through these three movements — Manifestation, Connection, and Illumination — life becomes a divine dialogue between heaven and earth, matter and light, human and divine.

1. THE LOWER TRIAD – THE FOUNDATION OF FORM
Root, Sacral, and Solar Plexus:
The Builders of Earthly Existence

This first triad anchors Spirit into matter. It is the realm of embodiment, movement, and creation — where the formless energy of consciousness learns to inhabit physical life. Here, love descends as vitality, as instinct, as the pulse that animates being.

- Root Chakra (Muladhara): Grounds consciousness in stability and survival. It teaches trust, belonging, and the sacredness of matter — the understanding that to be embodied is to be divine in form.

- Sacral Chakra (Svadhisthana): Awakens flow, creativity, and connection. Here, love becomes emotion in motion — the dance of relationship, desire, and joy that keeps life expanding.
- Solar Plexus Chakra (Manipura): Ignites will, confidence, and transformation. It is the fire that turns inspiration into action — love taking form through purposeful creation.

Together, these three form the Triad of Manifestation, where Spirit becomes matter and light anchors into life.
They are the roots through which heaven experiences earth — the vessel strong enough to hold light.

When balanced, this triad grants you stability, vitality, and agency — the strength to live, to create, and to act with conscious intent.
When imbalanced, it may express as fear, stagnation, or misuse of power — a reminder that true embodiment is an act of trust in life itself.

2. THE HEART – THE GREAT BRIDGE BETWEEN WORLDS
Where Spirit Descends and Soul Ascends

The Heart Chakra (Anahata) stands at the center of the human energy system — the still point where heaven and earth meet. It is the axis of the entire auric field, the sacred rhythm that unites what is above with what is below.

Through the Heart, the descending current of Spirit (from Crown to Root) and the ascending current of Soul (from Root to Crown) meet in perfect equilibrium. It is here that love becomes the harmonizing force — the language both matter and spirit understand.

The Heart teaches that:

- Power without compassion is empty.
- Vision without empathy is blind.
- Truth without kindness becomes distortion.

When the Heart is open, energy flows freely in both directions. It ensures that spiritual ascent never abandons the body, and material creation never forgets its source.

It whispers the secret of wholeness:

"As above, so below — as within, so without.
What is given through love returns through love."

Through the Heart, you remember that you were never divided — only exploring polarity for the sake of knowing unity.

3. THE UPPER TRIAD – THE ILLUMINATION OF CONSCIOUSNESS
Throat, Third Eye, and Crown: The Mirrors of Light

The upper triad refines experience into awareness and awareness into revelation. Here, energy ascends from expression to perception, from perception to unity — love becoming light, and light remembering itself as consciousness.

- Throat Chakra (Vishuddha): The voice of the soul — vibration refined into truth. Through sound, intention takes form; through silence, truth reveals its resonance.
- Third Eye Chakra (Ajna): The eye of wisdom — perception opening to divine vision. It is where the mind yields to intuition, and understanding replaces judgment.
- Crown Chakra (Sahasrara): The thousand-petaled lotus — pure awareness remembering itself. Here, all separation dissolves; the self expands into infinity; consciousness rests in its own eternal light.

Together, they form the Triad of Illumination, the ascending arc of evolution. Through them:

- Sound becomes silence.
- Perception becomes unity.
- Individuality dissolves into the field of pure being.

At this level, energy no longer strives to express or understand — it simply *is*. Awareness becomes luminous stillness; love becomes the very space through which all creation unfolds.

The Heart as the Great Equalizer

Between the foundation below and the illumination above, the Heart holds all in coherence.
It is the equalizer through which every energy center finds its rhythm, allowing heaven and earth to breathe as one.

When the chakras are harmonized through love:

- The Root feels safe enough to open.
- The Sacral flows without fear.
- The Solar Plexus acts without domination.
- The Throat speaks without distortion.
- The Third Eye sees without illusion.
- The Crown awakens without disconnection.

The result is not perfection — it is coherence.
Each chakra becomes a facet of the same diamond — the One Light expressing itself through seven hues of consciousness.

The Inner Path of Illumination

As energy rises from Throat to Third Eye to Crown:

- Doing softens into being.
- Expression matures into understanding.

- Understanding dissolves into presence.

Dreams become realization.
Intuition becomes trust.
Awareness becomes peace.

This is not the discovery of something new — it is the
remembering of what has always been.
Love no longer needs to speak or see — it simply is.

The Living Trinity Within You

The Lower Triad grounds light into matter.
The Upper Triad returns matter into light.
And the Heart — ever radiant, ever still — is the bridge through
which both meet in eternal embrace.

Together, they form the living trinity of human evolution:

- Manifestation (Earthly Life)
- Connection (Heart & Compassion)
- Illumination (Spiritual Awareness)

When these three movements are united, you become a conduit
of divine coherence — Spirit fully embodied, and humanity
fully enlightened.

"The Root holds the Light.
The Crown remembers the Earth.
And the Heart keeps them as one."

THE ALCHEMY OF CONSCIOUSNESS

Where the Throat carried truth outward and the Third Eye reflected it inward, the Crown radiates truth everywhere.
It is the still point through which creation breathes — the One in whom all opposites resolve.

The final alchemy:

- Sound → Silence
- Thought → Vision
- Vision → Light
- Light → Consciousness

At this level, there is no separation between the energy that creates, the one who perceives, and the consciousness that contains them both.

THE SEVEN ELEMENTS AS ONE SPECTRUM OF LIGHT

Element	Chakra	Function	How Sahasrara Unites It
Earth	Root	Structure	Becomes sacred foundation of embodiment
Water	Sacral	Flow	Becomes divine compassion and adaptability
Fire	Solar Plexus	Transformation	Becomes radiant will aligned with Spirit
Air	Heart	Connection	Becomes unconditional love beyond form
Ether	Throat	Expression	Becomes vibration returned to silence
Light	Third Eye	Perception	Becomes awareness beyond perception
Consciousness	Crown	Being	Becomes the field containing all creation

When all seven harmonize, the rainbow of the soul merges into white light — pure consciousness expressed as life.

The Unified Field – The Eternal Flow of Light and Form

INVOLUTION AND EVOLUTION AS ONE BREATH OF CREATION

In the Descent of Involution, Spirit moves into form — light becoming life.
In the Ascent of Evolution, life remembers itself as light.
Together, they form one continuous flow — the divine inhalation and exhalation of the cosmos.

Inhale: Spirit descends to experience itself.
Exhale: Matter releases itself back into Spirit.

This is the rhythm of existence itself — the pulse of the infinite expressed through every heartbeat, every breath, every unfolding moment.
It is the same current that animates galaxies and germinates seeds, rises through your spine, and blossoms at your crown.

You are not the traveler on this path — you are the path itself.
The luminous bridge between heaven and earth.
The consciousness through which creation breathes.

The Symphony of Being – How the Chakras Work Together

To understand Sahasrara, the thousand-petaled lotus of divine consciousness, you must see not only its brilliance above but also its roots below.
The crown cannot open without the earth beneath it; the light of heaven shines only through the form that holds it.

The chakras are not seven separate rungs of ascent, but seven tones in a single chord of being.

Each expresses a different octave of the same universal energy
— the music of Spirit awakening through matter.

- The Root grounds that music into life.
- The Sacral gives it movement and emotion.
- The Solar Plexus turns it into purposeful action.
- The Heart harmonizes every note through love.
- The Throat gives it resonance and expression.
- The Third Eye refines it into vision and wisdom.
- The Crown resolves it back into silence — unity beyond
  form.

Together, they create the harmonic resonance of being both
human and divine — the rainbow bridge of consciousness
through which Spirit experiences its own reflection.

The Circle of Creation

The journey of the chakras is not a ladder to climb, but a circle
of remembrance.
Energy does not simply rise — it flows continuously, in sacred
reciprocity, between heaven and earth.

- Descent (Involution): Light becomes matter — Spirit
  enters the world to know itself through creation.
- Ascent (Evolution): Matter becomes light — creation
  awakens to its own divinity and returns home to Source.

This is not two paths, but one eternal rhythm.
Spirit breathes into matter; matter exhales back into Spirit.
You are both inhale and exhale — both the expression and the
remembrance.

The human form is the temple through which consciousness
rediscovers its infinity.
You are the bridge where the Creator and the Created meet, the
meeting point of divine intention and human experience.

Integration Practice – The Vertical Breath of Unity

1. Sit comfortably, spine tall, feet grounded.
2. Inhale from the base of your spine to the crown — imagine light rising through each chakra like a golden river.
3. Pause at the crown, feeling your consciousness expand into infinite space — timeless, still, luminous.
4. Exhale from crown to root — bringing heaven's radiance back down into the earth, into your body, into life itself.
5. Rest awareness in the Heart, where both currents meet — heaven descending, earth ascending — the pulse of wholeness within you.

Repeat for seven breaths.
This is the Vertical Current of Unity — the embodied rhythm of Involution and Evolution, of love both descending and ascending.
You are breathing the cosmos, and the cosmos is breathing you.

The Path Forward – Integration of All That You Are

From Ajna, the journey rises to Sahasrara (Crown) — the remembrance of unity.
Through the Third Eye, you awaken awareness; through the Crown, you *embody* it.
The breath that began at the Heart now shines as pure consciousness.

You are no longer speaking your truth — you are being it.
You are no longer seeking guidance — you are becoming it.
Love now perceives itself through you.

When love becomes light, vision becomes truth.
When perception clears, the soul remembers what it has always been — divine awareness in motion.

At this final stage, the chakras no longer operate as separate centers, but as one seamless current of coherence — the rainbow bridge now returned to white light.
You have not left the world; you have illuminated it from within.
The descent and ascent are complete, and what remains is the gentle hum of creation resting in itself.

Final Reflection – The Thousand-Petaled Bloom

When the Crown opens, nothing new is gained — only remembered.
You realize that the entire journey, from Root to Crown, has always been the movement of one breath — one pulse of consciousness exploring itself through form.

All seven lights are one flame.
All seven sounds are one silence.
All seven lessons are one truth:

Love is the force that both creates and remembers.

When the chakras align, they form a single column of living light — a bridge between form and formlessness.
This is the awakened human — grounded, creative, empowered, loving, truthful, insightful, and free.

Sahasrara does not lift you away from life; it anchors you deeper into its holiness.
It reveals that the world itself was never apart from Spirit — it was Spirit in disguise, longing to see itself through you.

"All seven songs were always one melody.
The Crown does not rise above the Root — it blossoms because of it. The journey was never to escape the body, but to remember that consciousness has always been home."

Chapter 13 – Quick Reference Toolkit

Crown Chakra (Sahasrara)

THE CENTER OF UNITY, FAITH, AND DIVINE CONSCIOUSNESS

CORE OVERVIEW

Location: Top of the head or slightly above the crown (the "thousand-petaled lotus")
Element: Consciousness / Thought (beyond physical elements)
Color: Violet, white, or gold light
Bija Mantra: AUM / Silence (the sound beyond sound)
Governing Principle: Pure awareness and spiritual connection
Primary Function: Divine consciousness, enlightenment, faith, and unity with all life
Associated Glands/Organs: Pineal gland, cerebral cortex, upper brain, nervous system
Sense: Beyond the five senses — pure awareness or "knowing"
Astrological Associations: Uranus (awakening and transcendence) and the Sun (illumination and divine will)
Symbol: The thousand-petaled lotus — representing the infinite expansion of consciousness and union with the divine

KEY THEMES

• Unity, faith, and connection with Source
• Enlightenment and transcendence
• Trust in divine order and higher intelligence
• Grace, spiritual surrender, and cosmic consciousness
• Peace beyond understanding
• Integration of the self with all creation
• The awareness that all is One

WHEN BALANCED

• You feel deeply connected to life, others, and the divine.
• A natural sense of peace, gratitude, and reverence fills daily experience.
• Intuition flows effortlessly as divine guidance.
• You trust in life's timing and wisdom.
• Meditation feels expansive — awareness dissolves into stillness.
• You experience synchronicity and effortless alignment.
• Compassion arises spontaneously without effort or thought.

WHEN IMBALANCED

Underactive Crown (Deficient):
• Feelings of isolation, disconnection, or spiritual emptiness
• Cynicism or loss of faith in higher purpose
• Depression, confusion, or lack of inspiration
• Rigid thinking or over-identification with ego
• Difficulty accessing intuition or higher guidance

Overactive Crown (Excessive):
• Spiritual escapism or detachment from the physical world
• Over-intellectualizing spirituality without embodiment
• Feeling "ungrounded" or dissociated
• Head pressure, dizziness, or insomnia from energy overload
• Loss of discernment due to unanchored transcendence

BALANCING TECHNIQUES

Physical Practices:
• Gentle neck rolls, seated meditation postures, and Shavasana (Corpse Pose) for surrender
• Walking barefoot or grounding after meditation to integrate energy
• Head massages or acupressure at the crown and temples
• Sun-gazing at dawn or connecting with sky energy (briefly, eyes closed)

Energetic Practices:
• Violet or white light visualization expanding from the crown upward
• Silent meditation — focusing on spacious awareness rather than thoughts
• Reiki or energy work emphasizing connection with Source energy
• Prayer, devotion, or mantra chanting that invokes peace and surrender

Emotional / Spiritual Practices:
• Practice gratitude as a form of surrender and trust
• Meditate on "I Am" presence — the awareness behind thought
• Contemplation of unity ("We are all expressions of one divine essence")
• Mindful simplicity — living in quiet reverence for the ordinary moment

AROMATHERAPY & CRYSTALS

Essential Oils:
Frankincense – enhances connection with the divine
Myrrh – deepens meditation and spiritual reverence
Lotus – symbolizes enlightenment and divine grace
Lavender – calms the mind and harmonizes higher vibration
Rose – opens the heart to universal love and purity

Crystals:
Clear Quartz – amplifies consciousness and light
Amethyst – spiritual protection and awakening
Selenite – cleansing and connection to angelic realms
Lepidolite – serenity and emotional transcendence
Apophyllite – enhances meditation and divine communication

FOODS & NUTRITION

Supportive Foods:
• Light, high-vibration foods — fruits, herbal teas, fresh greens
• Coconut water or clear fluids for energetic purity
• Occasional fasting or mindful eating for clarity
• Spiritual herbs such as tulsi, lotus seed, or white sage tea

Avoid Excess:
• Heavy or overly processed foods that dull energy
• Intoxicants or stimulants that cloud perception
• Overeating or emotional eating that disconnects body–spirit awareness

AFFIRMATIONS

"I am one with the Divine Light that lives in all."
"I trust the wisdom of the universe flowing through me."
"I surrender to peace, love, and truth."
"My spirit is free, my heart is open, my mind is still."
"I am infinite awareness, eternal and whole."
"Through me, consciousness awakens to itself."

MUDRA & MANTRA

Mudra: *Sahasrara Mudra (Gesture of Enlightenment)*
– Interlace the fingers with palms facing upward; lightly touch the tips of the thumbs together.
– Hold above the crown or at heart level while breathing slowly.

– Opens higher consciousness and integrates light through the body.

Mantra: *AUM (Silence Beyond Sound)*
– Chant AUM softly, then allow the sound to fade into silence.
– Rest awareness in the stillness that follows — the true mantra of the Crown.
– Feel a radiant column of white-violet light connecting heaven and earth through you.

MEDITATION FOCUS

Visualize a soft violet or white light glowing at the top of your head.
With each breath, let it expand upward — an infinite lotus of light unfolding petal by petal.
Sense the light flowing through you, merging with the universe around you.
Rest in this vast awareness — not as a thought, but as pure being.

Repeat inwardly:

"I am light aware of itself.
I am peace beyond thought.
I am the stillness through which all creation flows."

Remain in silence.
Let the light dissolve boundaries — no inside, no outside — only presence.

INTEGRATION INSIGHT

Sahasrara is the crown of consciousness — the opening of your being to infinite unity.
It is where awareness recognizes itself as the Source of all, where the seeker and the sought become one.

When this chakra is balanced, life is no longer something to master — it becomes something to *revere*.
You act without attachment, love without condition, and see the divine in every form and circumstance.

The Crown teaches that enlightenment is not escape, but embodiment —
a surrender into the wholeness that has always been present.

"When awareness rests in the crown, there is no division, no striving.
There is only the quiet truth of being:
I Am That I Am — light, love, and consciousness eternal."

Conclusion: The Great Remembering

Conclusion of the Chakra 101 Series

FROM HEART TO ROOT TO CROWN — THE JOURNEY OF LOVE RETURNING TO LIGHT

Before the first breath, there was love.
Before the body formed, there was light.
And before thought could ask *Who am I?* — consciousness whispered, *I Am.*

You began this journey not to become divine, but to remember that you already are.
Each chakra has been a gate — a prism through which the One Light entered form to know itself through color, sensation, emotion, and thought.
But all the while, you were never separate from the Source you sought.
You were the pulse moving through every layer, the current of love descending into matter so that Spirit could experience its own reflection.

Through the Heart, you remembered compassion — the first echo of divine will expressed as life.
Through the Root, you remembered safety — love made tangible in earth and belonging.
Through the Sacral, you remembered movement — love learning the language of feeling and creation.
Through the Solar Plexus, you remembered power — love

discovering itself as purpose and transformation.
Through the Throat, you remembered truth — love becoming
vibration, shaping sound into existence.
Through the Third Eye, you remembered wisdom — love
seeing itself reflected in all.
And through the Crown, you remembered unity — love
dissolving back into the infinite field from which it was born.

Each center was not a step upward, but a spiral inward.
You have not climbed a ladder to heaven; heaven has bloomed
within you.
You are the axis where heaven and earth meet — the place
where form becomes formless, and formlessness takes form
again.

THE REVELATION OF WHOLENESS

There is no longer a seeker.
The seeker was the illusion that something was missing.
Now you see — it was love all along, discovering its own
reflection through the lens of time.

Every breath you take is the universe remembering itself.
Every heartbeat is Spirit saying, *I am still here.*
You are the continuity of God made visible —
the sacred breath returning to the silence from which it came.

Enlightenment is not escape; it is embodiment.
It is when awareness stops searching and begins to shine.
It is when light realizes it has never left the flame.

In this realization, duality melts — darkness reveals itself as
unlit light, silence as unspoken sound, and love as the truth
beneath all motion.

You are not the reflection in the mirror — you are the mirror,
the light, and the one who sees.

You are the awakening of consciousness through its own dream, and the dream awakening to itself as God.

THE INFINITE SPIRAL

The chakras no longer speak in seven tones.
Their colors merge — red into orange, orange into gold, gold into emerald, blue into violet — until all dissolve into white.
This is the return: the rainbow folding back into light.

The descent of Spirit into matter and the ascent of matter into Spirit were never two directions — they were the inhale and exhale of the same breath.
Inhale — the universe becomes you.
Exhale — you become the universe.
In this eternal rhythm, creation rests in recognition.

What you once called awakening is not the gaining of light, but the falling away of forgetting.
The final veil is memory — and when it lifts, you do not become divine. You remember that you were never anything else.

THE FINAL ILLUMINATION

Now stand at the still point — the thousand-petaled silence that blooms beyond becoming.
Here, all questions end because all answers dissolve into presence.
Here, the one who searches, the path that winds, and the goal ahead are revealed to be one and the same.

You are the love that became form so it could find itself again.
You are the word that became flesh so that sound could return to silence.
You are the light that traveled through color only to rediscover its whiteness.

"I am the pulse of creation,
the silence between the stars,
the light that dreams itself awake.
I am the beginning and the return —
the infinite remembering itself as Love."

And as this remembering unfolds, there is no end —
only the unbroken radiance of consciousness,
smiling through your eyes,
breathing through your heart,
living through your hands.

Welcome home.
You were never anywhere else.

Bibliography

CLASSICAL & YOGIC SOURCES

- Feuerstein, Georg. *The Yoga Tradition: Its History, Literature, Philosophy, and Practice.* Hohm Press, 2001.
- Avalon, Arthur (Sir John Woodroffe). *The Serpent Power: The Secrets of Tantric and Shaktic Yoga.* Dover Publications, 1974.
- Swami Sivananda. *The Chakras.* Divine Life Society, 1994.
- Easwaran, Eknath (trans.). *The Upanishads.* Nilgiri Press, 2007.
- Vivekananda, Swami. *Raja Yoga.* Advaita Ashrama, 1896. (Foundational text on concentration, meditation, and enlightenment.)
- Satyananda Saraswati, Swami. *Kundalini Tantra.* Bihar School of Yoga, 1984. (Explores Sahasrara as the thousand-petaled lotus and the union of Shiva–Shakti.)
- Paramahansa Yogananda. *Autobiography of a Yogi.* Self-Realization Fellowship, 1946. (Firsthand description of cosmic consciousness and samadhi.)
- Sri Aurobindo. *The Life Divine.* Sri Aurobindo Ashram Press, 1939. (A profound vision of evolution and divine realization.)
- Ramana Maharshi. *Be As You Are: The Teachings of Sri Ramana Maharshi.* Penguin, 1985. (Direct path to Self-realization through awareness.)

CHAKRA & ENERGY HEALING WORKS

- Judith, Anodea. *Wheels of Life: A User's Guide to the Chakra System.* Llewellyn Publications, 1987.
- Myss, Caroline. *Anatomy of the Spirit.* Harmony Books, 1996.
- Brennan, Barbara Ann. *Hands of Light: A Guide to Healing Through the Human Energy Field.* Bantam, 1988.
- Leadbeater, C. W. *The Chakras.* Quest Books, 1972. (Clairvoyant study of subtle energy and higher planes.)
- Dale, Cyndi. *The Subtle Body: An Encyclopedia of Your Energetic Anatomy.* Sounds True, 2009. (Comprehensive practitioner guide to multidimensional energy systems.)
- Santego, Constance. *Reiki Wisdom Series.* Maximillian Enterprises, 2024–. (Integration of Reiki consciousness, divine attunement, and vibrational mastery.)
- Stein, Diane. *Essential Reiki.* Crossing Press, 1995.
- Rand, William Lee. *Reiki: The Healing Touch.* Vision Publications, 1991.

REIKI, MEDITATION & SPIRITUAL SCIENCE

- Takata, Hawayo. *Reiki: Hawayo Takata's Story.* Reiki Alliance, 1998.
- Petter, Frank Arjava. *This Is Reiki.* Lotus Press, 2012.
- Dispenza, Joe. *Becoming Supernatural: How Common People Are Doing the Uncommon.* Hay House, 2017. (Meditation, quantum coherence, and unified field awareness.)
- Goswami, Amit. *The Self-Aware Universe.* Tarcher, 1995. (Quantum consciousness and non-duality.)
- Bentov, Itzhak. *Stalking the Wild Pendulum: On the Mechanics of Consciousness.* Destiny Books, 1977. (Bridges physics, vibration, and enlightenment states.)

PSYCHOLOGY, CONSCIOUSNESS & ENLIGHTENMENT

- Jung, Carl G. *The Archetypes and the Collective Unconscious.* Princeton University Press, 1969.
- Assagioli, Roberto. *Psychosynthesis: A Manual of Principles and Techniques.* Hobbs, Dorman & Co., 1965.
- Hillman, James. *The Soul's Code: In Search of Character and Calling.* Random House, 1996.
- Wilber, Ken. *A Brief History of Everything.* Shambhala, 1996. (Evolution of consciousness and integral spirituality.)
- Tolle, Eckhart. *The Power of Now.* New World Library, 1997. (Direct path to awakening through presence.)
- Tolle, Eckhart. *A New Earth: Awakening to Your Life's Purpose.* Penguin, 2005. (Transcendence of ego and realization of unity consciousness.)
- Chopra, Deepak. *The Book of Secrets: Unlocking the Hidden Dimensions of Your Life.* Harmony Books, 2004.
- Wilber, Ken. *The Spectrum of Consciousness.* Quest Books, 1977.
- Mooji. *Vaster Than Sky, Greater Than Space: What You Are Before You Became.* Sounds True, 2016. (Living realization of awareness beyond form.)

MYSTICAL & CROSS-CULTURAL TEXTS

- Rumi, Jalal al-Din. *The Essential Rumi.* Trans. Coleman Barks. HarperOne, 1995. (Poetic vision of unity with the Beloved.)
- Hanh, Thich Nhat. *The Miracle of Mindfulness.* Beacon Press, 1975.
- Ibn Arabi. *Journey to the Lord of Power.* Inner Traditions, 1981.
- Underhill, Evelyn. *Mysticism: A Study in the Nature and Development of Spiritual Consciousness.* Dover Publications, 2002.

- Campbell, Joseph. *The Hero with a Thousand Faces.* Princeton University Press, 1949.
- Sri Nisargadatta Maharaj. *I Am That.* Acorn Press, 1973. (Non-dual awareness as the essence of Sahasrara.)
- Krishnamurti, Jiddu. *The Awakening of Intelligence.* Harper & Row, 1973.
- Yogananda, Paramahansa. *God Talks with Arjuna: The Bhagavad Gita.* Self-Realization Fellowship, 1995. (Dialogue on union with the Divine.)
- Sadhguru. *Inner Engineering: A Yogi's Guide to Joy.* Spiegel & Grau, 2016.
- Adyashanti. *The End of Your World: Uncensored Straight Talk on the Nature of Enlightenment.* Sounds True, 2008.

MODERN SCIENCE & RESEARCH

- Lipton, Bruce H. *The Biology of Belief.* Hay House, 2005.
- McCraty, Rollin, et al. *Science of the Heart.* HeartMath Institute, 2015.
- Pert, Candace B. *Molecules of Emotion.* Scribner, 1997.
- Kauffman, Stuart. *At Home in the Universe.* Oxford University Press, 1995.
- Emoto, Masaru. *The Hidden Messages in Water.* Beyond Words, 2004.
- Grey, Alex. *The Mission of Art.* Shambhala, 1998. (Art as spiritual revelation — the language of the divine mind.)
- Hameroff, Stuart & Penrose, Roger. *Consciousness and the Universe: Quantum Physics, Evolution, Brain & Mind.* Cosmology Science Publishers, 2011.

ADDITIONAL RESOURCES

- Osho. *The Book of Secrets.* St. Martin's Griffin, 1998.
- Eden, Donna. *Energy Medicine.* TarcherPerigee, 2008.
- Hay, Louise. *You Can Heal Your Life.* Hay House, 1984.
- Blackstone, Judith. *Belonging Here: A Guide for the Spiritually Sensitive Person.* Sounds True, 2012.
- Wilber, Ken. *The Eye of Spirit.* Shambhala, 1997.
- Santego, Constance. *Reiki and the Five Elements.* Maximillian Enterprises, 2025. (Integration of natural elements with vibrational healing — foundational for crown embodiment.)

- Maharshi, Ramana. *Talks with Sri Ramana Maharshi.* Sri Ramanasramam, 1955.
- Chögyam Trungpa. *Cutting Through Spiritual Materialism.* Shambhala, 1973.
- Watts, Alan. *The Book: On the Taboo Against Knowing Who You Are.* Vintage, 1966.
- Bucke, Richard Maurice. *Cosmic Consciousness: A Study in the Evolution of the Human Mind.* Innes & Sons, 1901.

Message From The Author

By the time you reach this seventh and final book in the *Chakra 101 Series*, your energy has journeyed through every dimension of being — from the pulse of the heart to the infinite light of consciousness.

You began where all true healing begins — in the **Heart**, awakening unconditional love and divine remembrance.
You grounded that love through the **Root**, finding safety, belonging, and trust in the sacredness of Earth.
You allowed it to move through the **Sacral**, flowing as emotion, creativity, and relationship — love in motion.
You ignited it within the **Solar Plexus**, transforming will into courage, action, and luminous purpose.
You gave it **voice through the Throat**, learning that truth is not only spoken — it is vibrated into being.
You refined it in the **Third Eye**, where sound became light, and perception matured into wisdom.
And now, at the **Crown**, love completes its circle — dissolving into the brilliance of pure awareness.

This is not an ending, but a remembrance.
You are not ascending somewhere new — you are returning to what you have always been.
The chakras were never separate doors; they were facets of one radiant consciousness — seven mirrors through which the soul learns to recognize itself.

Through this journey, the seeker becomes the seen.
The light you have been seeking above has always lived within.
The silence you yearned for beyond the stars whispers now from inside your breath.

The **Crown Chakra** is not a place to arrive, but a realization to awaken:
that consciousness was never lost, only dreaming itself through form.
That the divine you prayed to has been experiencing itself
through your eyes, your voice, your heartbeat, your love.

You are not simply a student of the chakras —
you are their living expression.
You are the bridge where heaven and earth meet,
the spiral where love becomes light,
and light remembers itself as love.

May this final volume awaken in you the serene brilliance of the thousand-petaled lotus —
not as something to reach for, but as something blooming quietly within your crown.
May you live as one who walks in both worlds — rooted in peace, radiant with truth, and overflowing with compassion.
And may your every breath remind you that enlightenment was never the destination.
It is your natural state — the pure awareness that watches, loves, and creates through you.

With infinite gratitude, light, and love,
Dr. Constance Santego

About the Author

Dr. Constance Santego, Ph.D., DNM, is an internationally recognized natural medicine doctor, Grand Reiki Master, and bestselling author whose work bridges ancient spiritual wisdom with modern energy science. With more than twenty-five years of experience in holistic healing and education, she has trained thousands of students worldwide in Reiki, bioenergetics, intuitive development, and spiritual transformation.

As the founder of multiple wellness and educational programs, Dr. Santego has dedicated her life to teaching how energy, consciousness, and intention form the foundation of all true healing. Her passion lies in translating timeless truths into practical tools for awakening, empowerment, and self-mastery.

She is the author of over forty published works, including the acclaimed *Reiki Wisdom* series, *Secrets of a Healer* guides, and *The Nine Spiritual Gifts* novels — each uniting spirituality, science, and story to illuminate the path of soul evolution. Her *Chakra 101* series completes that vision: a journey of remembrance through seven gateways of transformation, where love descends into form and rises again as light.

Blending Eastern philosophy, Western natural medicine, and modern vibrational science, Dr. Santego's teachings center on compassion, coherence, and conscious awareness as the alchemy of wholeness. Her work invites seekers to go beyond knowledge into knowing — to awaken the inner healer, embody the divine, and remember their original light.

She resides in beautiful British Columbia, Canada, where the stillness of nature continues to inspire her writing, her practice, and her devotion to Spirit. Whether teaching in person or through her many books, Dr. Santego's message remains the same:

"You are not here to find the light — you are here to remember that you are the light."

This series was never meant to simply teach the chakras — it was written to awaken remembrance.
Each book, each lesson, each practice has been a thread in a greater tapestry: the soul's return to coherence, to love, to light.

The *Chakra 101 Series* began as a whisper — a call to guide others through the same unfolding I once walked. But as I wrote, I realized that this journey was not mine alone. It is humanity's — the story of consciousness remembering itself through the language of energy, the rhythm of breath, and the grace of awakening.

If these teachings have illuminated even one corner of your being, then the light continues to do its work.
May you carry this wisdom beyond the page — into your thoughts, your words, your touch, your world.

The path does not end here.
It expands — into new books, new modalities, new ways of remembering who we truly are.
May every step forward be a living expression of your awakened energy — grounded in love, guided by truth, and crowned with light.

With infinite gratitude,
Dr. Constance Santego

ALSO AVAILABLE

For additional information on

Constance Santego's

wide range of Motivational Products, Coaching Sessions,
Spiritual Retreats,
Live Events and Educational Programs

Go to

www.ConstanceSantego.ca

Follow on Instagram - Constance_Santego and
Facebook - constancesantegoo

Subscribe and receive Free Information and Meditations on her
YouTube Channel - Constance Santego

Secrets of a Healer, Magic of Reiki

ISBN: 978-1-7772220-0-0

Secrets of a Healer, The Reiki Master's Manual

ISBN: 978-1-990062-34-6

www.ingramcontent.com/pod-product-compliance
Lightning Source LLC
Chambersburg PA
CBHW071708120626
46550CB00001B/152